IMAGES OF

THE LONG RANGE DESERT GROUP IN ACTION 1940-1943

RARE PHOTOGRAPHS FROM WARTIME ARCHIVES

Brendan O'Carroll

Pen & Sword
MILITARY

First published in Great Britain in 2020 and reprinted in 2021 by
PEN & SWORD MILITARY
An imprint of
Pen & Sword Books Ltd
Yorkshire – Philadelphia

ISBN 978-1-52677-741-6

Typeset by Concept, Huddersfield, West Yorkshire, HD4 5JL
Printed and bound in England by CPI Group (UK) Ltd, Croydon CR0 4YY

Pen & Sword Books Limited incorporates the imprints of Atlas, Archaeology, Aviation, Discovery, Family History, Fiction, History, Maritime, Military, Military Classics, Politics, Select, Transport, True Crime, Air World, Frontline Publishing, Leo Cooper, Remember When, Seaforth Publishing, The Praetorian Press, Wharncliffe Local History, Wharncliffe Transport, Wharncliffe True Crime and White Owl.

For a complete list of Pen & Sword titles please contact
PEN & SWORD BOOKS LIMITED
47 Church Street, Barnsley, South Yorkshire, S70 2AS, England
E-mail: enquiries@pen-and-sword.co.uk
Website: www.pen-and-sword.co.uk
or
PEN AND SWORD BOOKS
1950 Lawrence Rd, Havertown, PA 19083, USA
E-mail: Uspen-and-sword@casematepublishers.com
Website: www.penandswordbooks.com

Contents

Acknowledgements

This book would not exist if it were not for the kindness and generosity of a number of like-minded military historians, veterans and their families, researchers, collectors and authors who shared their research material and photos. Listed further are the names of the many who contributed to help create this photographic tribute to the Long Range Desert Group.

I wish to thank Jonathan Pittaway of South Africa, the author of two books on the LRDG: *LRDG Rhodesia* (2002) and *Long Range Desert Group, Rhodesia: The Men Speak* (2009). He has kindly shared the Rhodesian S Patrol images published in this book and has been very supportive of my publications over the years.

Also thanks to Ian Chard from England, LRDG researcher and Y Patrol historian. He has been a wonderful contributor, providing copies of LRDG photos and other related research documents from British LRDG veterans. The Y Patrol images, via Ian, came from the wartime albums of Brian and Marjorie Springford, Harry Chard, Tich Cave and Mick Allen. Ian was always helpful and very responsive in answering my many queries or offering information.

Thanks to my wife Margaret for her kind assistance and patience with logistics and proofreading skills, and to my children, Diana, Michelle and Patrick, for their continued support with resolving computer processes and technical issues, photography and general advice.

Thanks to my photo restorer Nick Hofmann for his skill, time and patience in enhancing up some of the poorer images, as civilian wartime film developing in dirty Cairo water had left much dust, dirt and fluff on the original personal album photographs.

A special acknowledgement goes to the New Zealand LRDG veterans, listed below, who over my twenty years of research kindly shared their memories with me; also in allowing me generous access to their private wartime photograph albums, along with permission to publish the images as a tribute to their LRDG comrades. All of these men have now passed on, but their stories remain in image and word.

The veterans include Denis Bassett, Merlyn Craw, Merv Curtis, Merle Fogden, Les Nicholls, Peter Garland, Buster Gibb, Ian Gold, Ray and Erl Gorringe, Basil Green-street, Don Gregory, Jack Job, Ian Judge, Fred Kendall, Dick Lewis, Sam Lucas, Charles McConachie, Ian McCulloch, Peter McGregor, Les Middlebrook, Tom Ritchie, Alf Saunders, Keith Tippett, Richard Williams, Wally Rail, Clarke Waetford, Bill Whimp, Frank White, Bill Willcox, Alex Yaxley.

Finally, my thanks to the many other contributors, including fellow researchers and LRDG widows and family members, who also provided photos and reference material, along with their time and interest. Furthermore, I apologize to any I may have overlooked, as over my many years of writing the names of some individual contributors may have been lost. I have made my best efforts to include all, and to acknowledge their support in sharing images, permissions, etc. Without the help of so many people, it would have been impossible to present this visual record of the LRDG adequately. Thanks to the following: Peter and Rosemary Beech, Ricardo Brennan, Leighton Burne, Bain and Dorothy Cross, David Ellis, the Fogden family, Amanda Gill, Andrew Honeyfield, Jenny Hughes, Ken Johnson, Irene Jopling, John Leonard, Ngaire Lewis, Jason and Nik Magerkorth, Liz McNeil, Ethan O'Carroll, Sharon Palmer, Shirley Patten, Matthew Rice, Antonio Maraziti, Jeremy Riley, Bill Saxton, Eric, John and Michael Shepherd, Lucie Stokes, Emily Subritzky, Isabelle Subritzky, Nick Szalardi, David Thompson, John (Jack) Valenti, Charlie Waetford, Warner Wilder, Eric Wilson and Ronny Yavin.

Introduction

This is an overview tale of the Long Range Desert Group (LRDG) told through images and explanatory captions. The journey through wartime photos starts with its formation in July 1940 until the end of 1943, after which the unit was re-established and transformed into a Commando-type role serving in Europe until the end of the war.

It is set out introducing the founding unit in the early days, the Long Range Patrol (LRP). From there it progresses to the formation of the Long Range Desert Group and their first significant behind-the-lines operation in the Fezzan region, southern Libya. The next chapters cover the vehicles, weapons, equipment and activities from when the specially desert-adapted CMP Fords and 1942 Chevrolets were used, between 1941 and 1943. The LRDG Air Section is also presented. The famed Barce Raid in September 1942 is described in a photo narrative and from there follows a pictorial overview of the closing days in the desert. The Dodecanese operations in the Aegean in late 1943 embody the final images.

The story is told in the chapter introductions and captions and begins with the unit's initial purpose of travelling long distances behind enemy lines in Libya on intelligence-gathering, mapping and reconnaissance missions; hence they were first known as the Long Range Patrols, manned by New Zealanders and British officers. In December 1940 the British Guards joined and it then became the Long Range Desert Group. Soon after, they were reinforced by troops from Southern Rhodesia and British Yeomanry regiments who formed their own individual patrols.

This work is not intended to be a concise history of the LRDG as many other publications have already provided that. Rather the images are presented to serve as a general reference to the type of vehicles used, including the weapons and equipment, the sort of aircraft they flew, the landscape travelled, some personalities and uniform and insignia. There are also views of enemy action, results of LRDG-placed ambushes, the taking of prisoners, attacks on airfields and forts and working with the SAS.

Photo stories will cover the early raids in the Fezzan in southern Libya January 1941, plus the famous Barce Raid in the north in September 1942. Furthermore, everyday life, meals, camping, hunting, the dropping off of agents, rescuing downed airmen, treating the wounded and getting stuck in the sand are also portrayed. These will allow the reader an insight into the tough yet rewarding life of an LRDG patrolman operating in one of the most harsh terrains and climates in the world. These images can also serve as a useful reference for researchers of Special Forces, militaria collectors and re-enactors, military modellers and vehicle restorers, plus as art department guides in film and television.

When the desert war was over in May 1943, the LRDG reorganized their force in the Cedars of Lebanon. Now without their specialized vehicles, they continued their intelligence-gathering role and trained as small covert, independent foot reconnaissance patrols.

In September 1943, they were sent to the Dodecanese Islands in the Aegean as coast-watchers, to assist a British brigade and their new Italian allies in holding the islands against the Germans. However, after three months and the final five days of the Battle of Leros, the situation turned into a defeat. The Germans had total dominance of the air and eventually overwhelmed the British and Italian garrison troops who were forced to surrender. The LRDG was serving independently, but had tragically lost more men after three months on the islands than after three years in the desert. Consequently, the New Zealand patrols, who were the founding troops of the group, were disbanded and returned to their original units. This photo story ends with that. The British and Rhodesian patrols continued to serve in Europe in a Commando/intelligence-gathering role until the end of the war.

Most of the images are from 'unofficial' personal cameras carried by individuals. Strictly speaking this was against regulations, but the LRDG tended to do things their own way and the rule was not enforced. Thus thankfully today, a reader can enjoy the LRDG story through the lens of a trooper. The only downside is that the personal cameras were not of a high quality; hence the images tend not to be as sharp or as clean as those of an official army photographer. There are a number of high-quality 'official' LRDG photos that are often seen repeated in LRDG publications over the years. However, with this work, for the most part I have avoided using those, preferring to utilize the lesser-known personal LRDG images to tell the story.

Furthermore, much of the film was developed in Cairo photo shops, where the water used in the process was often unclean so the images appeared with specks of dust and dirt, hairs and even insect wings! Also, with the cameras being carried on long patrols, usually in a web pack, they were exposed to heat and dust, being bounced around in the back of a truck. This would therefore impact on the quality of the final print, which often suffered scratches from dust in the unexposed film and areas of heat or light exposure on the print. Many of these I have had cleaned up to present a tidier image. Nonetheless, regardless of the quality, the LRDG veterans filled their photo albums with these memories and showed them off with great pride.

Many of the photos reflect the New Zealand R and T patrols. This is because my main source of images was from those veterans. However, the Rhodesian S Patrol, the Guards G Patrol and Yeomanry Y Patrol are also represented. Despite this New Zealand prominence, the vehicles, weapons, equipment and activities were universal among the patrols, the only difference being the personnel and truck names and numbers.

It was normal practice to share the photos taken among the patrol members. Consequently, when I viewed veterans' wartime albums, the same photos would often appear. So it is virtually impossible to establish who was the original photographer to give due credit, though Trooper Frank Jopling of T Patrol took many photos and shared them with his comrades, as did others. In the Acknowledgements section I have given a general credit to the veterans and others who provided images for me to publish over the last twenty years. Many of these have already appeared in some of my previous six LRDG-related books, but are now compiled into one reference. The veterans and families I encountered were pleased to share their photos with the world as they bring to life the narrative of these great men and their adventures in North Africa and the Aegean. They will serve as a unique visual tribute to one of the first Special Forces of the Second World War.

Brendan O'Carroll
2020

Chapter One

The Early Days

The war in North Africa came to an end with the Axis surrender in May 1943. While the opposing armies had advanced and retreated along the Mediterranean coast, Long Range Desert Group patrols had for almost three years operated behind enemy lines, dominating the vast inner deserts of Egypt, Libya and Tunisia.

The Long Range Desert Group had its beginnings in July 1940, when Major Ralph Bagnold conceived the unit. He was a British army signals officer, geographer and desert explorer. Following the Italian entry into the war in June 1940, Egypt was now considered under threat as Libya had been an Italian colony since the 1920s. Consequently, the British Middle East GHQ needed urgent intelligence as to the enemy activity in southern Libya close to the Egyptian border.

Bagnold, along with a small group of fellow explorers, had ventured into Libya in the 1920s and 1930s and acquired considerable knowledge on desert travel, navigation and survival techniques. Armed with these abilities, he offered his services to General Sir Archibald Wavell, C-in-C Middle East, to lead a patrol far behind the lines and establish the Italian dispositions and intentions. With southern Libya well beyond the range of aerial observation, he immediately authorized Bagnold's plans for an overland reconnaissance unit to be formed, with six weeks to recruit and prepare the force – officially titled the No. 1 Long Range Patrol Unit (also known as the LRP).

Its first volunteers answered a call which specified men 'who do not mind a hard life, scanty food, little water, lots of discomfort, and possess stamina and initiative.' Consequently, for the first six months of its operations the LRP was manned almost entirely by specially selected members from the Second New Zealand Expeditionary Force (2NZEF). These men had been training in Egypt since their arrival in early 1940 and were available for attachment. Because the initial long-range reconnaissance patrols had proved their worth, it was decided to continue and expand the force. In December 1940, recruits from the Coldstream and Scots Guards regiments joined the unit, which then became known as the Long Range Desert Group. Later further reinforcements came from Southern Rhodesian and the British Yeomanry regiments. They became one of the first Special Forces of the Second World War.

The LRDG comprised individual patrols; W, R and T being the New Zealand patrols with their vehicles bearing Maori names beginning with that letter. The others were the Guards (G), Yeomanry (Y) and the Southern Rhodesians (S). At the start, these consisted of twenty-seven to thirty-two men travelling in eleven special desert-adapted vehicles. The first issue was 1939 Model Chevrolet WB trucks. They were led by a commander's pilot vehicle, a Ford 01 V8 15cwt.

A headquarters unit oversaw the patrols and was supported by a signals, survey and light repair sections. In addition, there was a Heavy Section (trucks for logistical support) that was employed to transport supplies to bases and to establish forward hidden dumps, which helped to extend the range of operations to great distances.

Ground reconnaissance was the principal objective of the Group, to provide by way of patrols detailed charting and information about enemy dispositions from deep behind the lines in the Libyan desert. This small but extremely effective force of British and Empire troops ran reconnaissance and survey patrols with great regularity from Cairo to Tripoli over some of the most challenging and arid terrain in the world. Each patrol was a completely self-contained independent body, capable of travelling hundreds of kilometres deep into enemy territory over all types of difficult desert landscape. They were experts in navigation, desert survival and warfare. This was only possible due to their well-maintained and special desert-modified trucks. These vehicles were skilfully driven and navigated by tough, self-reliant men who adapted well to desert life with its extreme climatic and geographical conditions.

Apart from reconnaissance trips and setting up forward dumps, the LRP's first direct-action role was to place mines on the roads used by Italian convoys or to lay ambush against them. While undertaking such an operation in October 1940, Captain D.G. Steele's R Patrol found an enemy bomb dump buried in the sand. More than 700 bombs were dug up and destroyed. Later the same day they burned an unguarded Savoia-Marchetti S.79 bomber and 160 drums of fuel.

Meanwhile, Captain P.A. Clayton's T Patrol had laid mines on the Jalo-Ajedabia road and distributed pamphlets written in Arabic inciting the tribes to make trouble in Libya. On 1 November 1940, the column attacked a small Italian fort at Aujila, where after the first burst of machine-gun fire and rounds from the truck-mounted 37mm Bofors gun, the astonished garrison ran off to a nearby native village. Clayton captured two machine guns, rifles and stores, along with one Libyan soldier for interrogation.

Between 28 October and 4 November 1940, the LRP worked with the RAF to undertake mapping and reconnoitre for possible landing grounds. An obsolete Vickers Valentia from No. 216 (Bomber Transport) Squadron RAF was employed to carry out this work. The aircraft was fitted with long-range tanks and was refuelled from three dumps previously laid by the LRP for that specific purpose. It had a crew of six who worked in liaison with Captain E.C. Mitford and the medical officer Captain F.B. Edmundson of the LRP. Because of load concerns it was impossible to carry enough water for the whole operation, so it was supplied by the ground patrols when they made contact with the aircraft.

With the aid of the Valentia, more topographical information was obtained about the recently-found Kalansho Sand Sea. In other areas, the 'going' was plotted for future mapping and further landing grounds were located. The aircraft flew eight missions that covered a distance of 3,070 kilometres, with a total flying time of nearly twenty-five hours. They were lucky they had not encountered enemy aircraft that would have made short work of such a slow lumbering target.

In late November, led by Captain E.C. Mitford, W Patrol visited Uweinat where for over an hour they were attacked by three enemy aircraft. Though many small bombs were dropped, skilful, evasive driving resulted in no damage being done. The patrol then went on to the Italian outpost at Ain Dua, which at first appeared deserted. A round from the 37mm Bofors gun was fired, which brought an immediate response of enemy rifle and machine-gun fire. The garrison, estimated to be thirty men with three machine guns, was well-established in among large boulders, stone walls and trenches. Consequently, a frontal attack over an open plain was not an option.

Lieutenant J.H. Sutherland commanded D Troop, consisting of three trucks and eight men. They moved against the enemy's left flank, while the rest of the patrol gave covering fire. The troop worked its way through the rocks on foot. Yet despite coming under steady fire, they managed to drive the Italians up the hill into fresh positions, leaving three casualties, including one dead.

Two Italian bombers, then later a reconnaissance plane appeared overhead, so the patrol quickly withdrew and hid among the rocks. After several hours the sky was clear again and a second attack on Ain Dua was launched. The plan was to attack from both flanks while still covered from the centre. With its Bofors gun in support, D Troop attacked over the ground where it had been before. While one truck and a Bofors gun gave covering fire from the plain, the rest of the patrol worked their way around the right flank. Sutherland reached the edge of the fortifications and inflicted casualties from grenades launched from an EY grenade-launching rifle, but he was then pinned down by return fire.

Trooper L.A. Willcox crawled with his .303 Lewis gun to within 18 metres of an enemy machine-gun emplacement, stood up, fired his weapon from the hip and killed the crew of four. Sutherland moved in closer, but he was again cut off by enemy fire. Willcox came to his rescue a second time by silencing a further machine-gun position.

Owing to the almost impassable massive rocks, the remainder of the patrol was unable to get close enough to engage the Italians. The garrison was well-placed and defended themselves so capably that it was impossible to take the position without incurring heavy losses. Accordingly at dusk, W Patrol withdrew, leaving six of the enemy killed and at least six wounded without taking any casualties themselves. As a result of this action, Sutherland received the first Military Cross and Willcox the first Military Medal awarded to the LRP.

Members of the NZ Divisional Cavalry rest in their tent at Maadi Camp, Egypt in May 1940. Left: Lance Corporal D.J. Adams, Trooper J. Davies, Trooper P.L. Garland and Corporal F.R. Beech. These men all volunteered to join the Long Range Patrol (LRP) formed in July 1940. Beech was later killed in action.

One of the two civilian-purchased Chevrolet WB trucks used on the first LRP incursion into Libya, August 1940. Captain P.A. Clayton, with six New Zealanders and an Arab servant, successfully undertook a nine-day reconnaissance trip into Libya. They successfully travelled without a radio, sand mats or trays and armed with only two .303 Lewis machine guns.

The first patrols loading boxed supplies at their base at Abbassia, Cairo in 1940.

T Patrol at Abbassia ready to move off on a mission, with truck *Te Anau* T10 in the foreground. The New Zealand patrol trucks all carried Maori names beginning with the letter of the patrol.

The first two NZ Patrol commanders, Abbassia, 1940. Left: Lieutenant L.B. Ballantyne, T Patrol and Lieutenant D.G. Steele, R Patrol. They are driving the R Patrol 1938 Ford 01 15cwt V8 pilot (command) car. These vehicles led the early patrols.

Lieutenant Steele's Ford V8 deeply stuck in liquid sand while crossing the Sand Sea, September 1940. Note the R Patrol pennant, plus the aero compass below the driver's seat, also the EY grenade-launching rifle next to the pith helmet.

The 1939 Chevrolet WB 4 × 2 30cwt R Patrol truck *Rotowaro*. It was unusual to see the canvas hood in place. Though it provided good shade, it restricted the driver's aerial view and was soon discarded. The wooden Shell 'flimsy' fuel tin cases are stacked high in the rear. Also the headlights are covered to prevent reflection.

A profile view of an R Patrol Chevrolet WB in a rocky landscape on the road to Zouar. Note the steel sand channels hung on the side.

A Chevrolet WB being cleaned out after a small fire in the back. With all the fuel carried in leaky tins, the risk of fire by accident or from the enemy was always present.

An unusual view of the inside of a Chevrolet WB. The troops called the wooden-framed space the 'pig pen'. It was being cleaned out as a result of a small fire. Note the covered .55 Boys anti-tank rifle mounted on a steel crossbar.

Chevrolet WB ploughing over a sand dune. It was not unusual for a vehicle to get stuck on the top or overturn while cresting a dangerous razorback dune.

A panoramic view of T Patrol assembling after crossing a sand sea.

Trooper R.J. Landon-Lane standing next to his Chevrolet WB, R2, *Rotowhero*. The early trucks carried War Department and Egyptian number plates, but these were soon discarded as the rigours of desert travel knocked them about. The vehicle mounts a Lewis gun and a Boys anti-tank rifle.

A desert vista: patrol tracks seen through some of the most spectacular desert rock formations and landscapes encountered on their travels.

An R Patrol truck crew view petrified trees in the desert. See how defined their vehicle tracks are in the stony sand.

To provide forward supply dumps to enable the patrols to extend their missions, the Heavy Section was created. Here is the first HS unit posing in front of their 6-ton Ford Marmon-Herrington truck. From left to right: Trooper J. Zimmerman, Trooper F.D. Rhodes, Sergeant A.W. Hood, Private A.F. McLeod, Lieutenant W.B. Kennedy Shaw (navigator), Private E.T. Russell and Lance Corporal J.L. Schaab. The rum jar was an essential evening tonic on every patrol.

A Marmon-Herrington, HS truck bogged in the sand. It was carrying petrol to the dump at Ain Dalla, Egypt.

Driven by Trooper J. Zimmerman, a Marmon-Herrington travels at speed over good terrain. Note the extra long sand channels and the engine side bonnet panels removed for cooling.

Camp supplies and cooking arrangements. Most supplies were packed in wooden boxes to enable efficient packing within the trucks.

Trucks negotiating the difficult basalt rock terrain west of Uau an-Namus. This landscape had to be crossed slowly in low gear, as it could lead not only to punctures but cracked sumps, exhaust systems or differential housings.

The patrols were experts in camouflage and have employed a depression in the rocky ground for cover.

The massive boulders in the Uweinat region. The Italians had an outpost there at Ain Dua, which W Patrol under Captain E.C. Mitford attacked in November 1940. As a result of this action, Lieutenant J.H. Sutherland received the first Military Cross and Trooper L.A. Willcox the first Military Medal awarded to the LRP/LRDG.

W Patrol members from left: Trooper J.W. Eyles (navigator), Corporal F.R. Beech (later killed at Jebel Sherif on 31 January 1941) and Sergeant A.D. Gibb. All are armed with pistols. The cooker on the ground is made from an old drum.

A semi-permanent camp site during the siege at Giarabub, March 1941. Erected beside the truck *Rotokawa* is a tarpaulin providing comfortable shade for the men. The supplies and cooking arrangements are well spread out.

Giarabub 1941. Y Patrol members, well-tanned in summer dress, stand in front of their camp shelter. From left: Trooper H.C. Chard, Trooper R.H. Lee and Trooper J.D. Hirst. Note Harry Chard is wearing an Italian bayonet. Later he was captured by the Afrika Korps on 13 January 1942 while with Y1 Patrol watching a fort at Marada.

Captain Steele with members of R Patrol poses with a barrel of brandy captured from the Italians, plus their own rum jars. This resulted for a time in some heavy drinking around the camp fires at night.

R Patrol *Rotowai* R4 sleeping arrangements. Private E.T. Russell rests against an unrolled sand mat. This served as an effective headboard and shelter from the wind.

Italian supply convoy of the Saharan Tractor Company intercepted and destroyed by the LRP.

The results of an LRP convoy raid, with cargo trailers burning in the background.

A Chevrolet WB truck mounting a 37mm Bofors anti-tank gun. One of these was attached to each patrol.

Some of the first prisoners captured by the LRP, mainly Libyans working for the Italians as drivers, September 1940.

A member of T Patrol poses behind an Austrian-made Schwarzlose M1907/12 heavy machine gun. It was taken from the captured Italian fort at Aujila on 1 November 1940.

An Italian Lancia truck disabled by mines, 1941. R Patrol members, from left: Sergeant P. McGregor, Trooper L.A. Willcox and Sergeant A.D. (Buster) Gibb. Behind the truck were the remains of an Italian killed by the blast.

The men relaxing with their books. The truck is camouflaged with scrim hessian fabric. This was later replaced with netting, which was more effective as the hessian stood out in the landscape. The .303 Lewis gun is at the ready in case of an air attack. Left: Trooper M.E. Hammond, Private E. Harcourt and Private M. Allen (RAMC medical orderly).

The same men display their woolly Hebron goat or sheepskin coats, used as protection against the cold.

T Patrol men dressed against the wind chill. Left: Signalman A. Pressick (Royal Corps of Signals), Trooper E.W.R. Kitney, Corporal L.H. (Tony) Browne and Lieutenant L.B. Ballantyne.

R Patrol members – left, Troopers C. Waetford and J.W. Eyles – boiling water to wash their towels. The wood from broken petrol boxes fuel the fire. Empty 4-gallon flimsy tins could be recycled as cooking, carrying and washing containers. The heavy .303 Vickers machine gun is mounted on the truck, uncovered ready for action.

Private E.T. Russell poses alongside his truck. On the running board is a 2-gallon tin that serves as a water condenser, with the recycling tube running to the radiator. The three small packs behind the driver's compartment are the crew 'bail out' kits. These contained emergency rations, a compass, water bottle and cigarettes. The packs were placed for easy access in case the vehicle had to be abandoned in a hurry.

Lance Corporal A. Pressick, a British signalman of the Royal Corps of Signals attached to T Patrol, February 1941. In the Chevrolet WB, the radio was fitted inside the rear of the truck. In the later vehicles, it was accessed from the outside. Behind him, mounted on a steel crossbar, is the bolt-action .55 Boys anti-tank gun. It held a five-round magazine and was rarely employed against the enemy.

A regular challenge while operating in soft sand. Before placing the steel sand channels to extract the vehicle, the men had to dig out the sand first. It mounts a .55 Boys anti-tank rifle and Lewis gun.

R Patrol Chevrolet WB with the crew warmly dressed. Note the Maori *Tiki* symbol on the bonnet. This indicated an R Patrol vehicle, whereas T Patrol displayed a Kiwi. The lights and windscreens were covered with cloth to prevent sun reflection.

An LRDG medical orderly applies first-aid alongside R8, *Rotoehu*. All patrols included medical orderlies, who also served as fighting soldiers.

Very tanned R Patrol members in a Libyan village; some are wearing army leather jerkins.

Corporal G.C. Garven of T Patrol displaying the .303 EY grenade-launching rifle. They were used effectively on a number of occasions against enemy positions, most notably when Y2 Patrol attacked a small Italian fort at El Ezzeiat. A grenade was skilfully projected by Trooper B.C. Springford at a machine-gun tower. The occupants were killed and it led to the surrender of the fort with twenty prisoners taken.

An RAF Vickers Valentia troop carrier flies over an LRP radio truck. To the right of the vehicle is an erected Wyndom aerial, which much improved communications over long distances.

The Vickers Valentia with T Patrol members posing in front, October 1940. In conjunction with the LRP, this obsolete aircraft flew eight missions for mapping and reconnaissance work with the patrols in support.

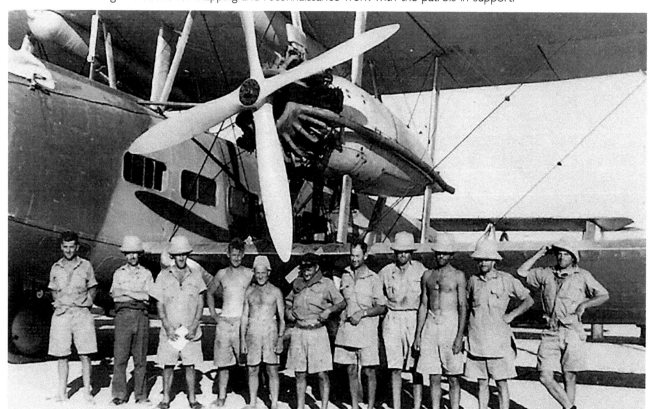

Troopers H.D. (Paddy) Mackay (left) and J.L.D. Davis plot their position with the aid of a theodolite. Note the unusual leather pistol holster and rig.

PLATE III.
The Bagnold Navigating Sun Compass.

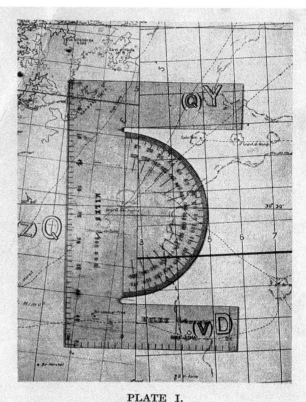

PLATE I.
LRDG pattern protractor correctly set by eye square with latitude and longitude graticule, the grid being disregarded

(**Above, left**) Bagnold's sun compass, the key LRDG daytime navigation tool. Using the shadow cast by the sun on the compass rose, it indicated the bearing on which the vehicle was travelling. These images are from the military manual used by the LRDG, *Field Navigation, Part 1. Dead Reckoning* (February 1942).

(**Above, right**) LRDG pattern protractor used for plotting a course.

(**Right**) Azimuth card used in conjunction with the sun compass.

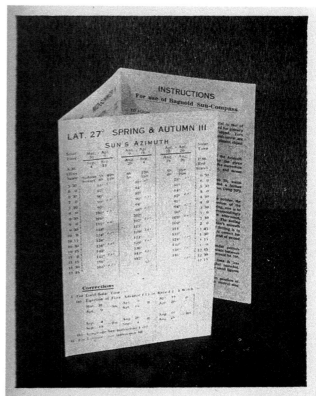

PLATE IV.
Azimuth Card for use with Bagnold Navigating Sun Compass.

Chapter Two

LRDG Operations in the Fezzan, 1941

The first large-scale LRDG operation began with the introduction of the Guards Patrol in December 1940. W Patrol was disbanded and their 1939 Chevrolet WB 30cwt trucks and equipment went to G Patrol. The LRP men were absorbed in R and T Patrols or returned to their original units to fight in Greece and later Crete. In conjunction with the Free French Forces (*Forces françaises libres*, FFL) of Chad Province, the LRDG set out on 26 December on a series of raids on the Italian garrisons of the Fezzan, in south-west Libya. The main objective was the town and airfield of Murzuk, the capital of the region, which was 2,150 kilometres from Cairo and 560 kilometres from the nearest French post in the Tibesti Mountains. They were commanded by Major P.A. Clayton, a 1930s' desert explorer, who led seventy-six men of G and T Patrols in a column of twenty-four vehicles. Captain M.D. Crichton-Stuart commanded the Guards, while Lieutenant L.B. Ballantyne acted as second-in-command to Major Clayton, who travelled with the New Zealanders.

To keep their intentions secret, they avoided the routes that led to wells and oases. Clayton left the patrols at a rendezvous about 240 kilometres to the north and took four trucks to Kayugi in the foothills of the Tibesti Mountains. There he collected Lieutenant Colonel J.C. d'Ornano, the flamboyant commander of the FFL in Chad. He was accompanied by Captain Massu and Lieutenant Eggenspiller, two sergeants and five native troops.

On 11 January 1941, the now combined force reached the road running south-wards from Sebha to Murzuk, which they mined. After stopping for lunch, Major Clayton led the patrols in his Ford V8 *Te Rangi* towards the fort at Murzuk. Along the way a group of Libyans, mistaking them for Italians, gave the Fascist salute. A postman, overtaken while cycling to the fort, was picked up and forced into the leading truck to supply information and act as a guide. His bicycle was also taken and hooked on the back of Corporal F.R. Beech's truck.

The garrison, some of whom were outside the gates of the fort, had been taken completely by surprise as they received machine-gun fire from the trucks. Clayton branched off and led a troop of T Patrol towards the airfield, while the remainder deployed to engage the fort with the Guards' Bofors gun, 2in mortars and machine guns. The defenders soon recovered from their shock and offered stubborn resistance, returning heavy fire. As Sergeant C.D. Hewson stood up in his truck *Te Hau* to clear his machine gun, a bullet ricocheted off the bonnet and struck him in the heart. He was the first LRDG man to be killed in action.

The fort was now successfully contained and a 2in mortar bomb fired by Trooper I.H. McInnes hit a petrol drum that set the tower ablaze. He was later awarded the Military Medal for his effective mortar-shooting. During the attack a staff car drove up to the gate transporting the garrison commander but, unbeknown to the LRDG at the time, it also carried his wife and children. The vehicle was hit by Bofors and machine-gun fire and the occupants killed.

In the meantime, six trucks attacked the airfield firing their Bofors and machine guns, targeting the pillboxes and gun pits. Major Clayton, who was accompanied by Colonel d'Ornano, drove off to encircle the hangar, but as he turned the corner they encountered a machine-gun post at close range. Unfortunately the Ford's Vickers gun had jammed and before they could reverse, d'Ornano was fatally wounded in the throat. An Italian prisoner was also killed.

The troops continued to fire at the hangar until its defenders surrendered, with twenty-five prisoners being taken. The building, which contained three Ghibli aircraft, bombs, parachutes, radio equipment and other stores, was soaked in petrol and set alight, although anything useful was taken beforehand, like the recovery of thousands of rounds of .303 ammunition in Lewis gun pans. These weapons were used by air gunners in the Ghiblis.

Although the airfield had been captured, the garrison in the fort still held out. Nonetheless, the purpose of the raid had been achieved in the destruction of the airfield, so after two hours of fighting, Clayton withdrew his patrols. It was estimated that ten of the enemy were killed and fifteen wounded. The LRDG/FFL force suffered two killed and five wounded. Of the twenty-five prisoners taken, all except an Air Force officer and the postman were released due to a lack of transport space and rations. The bodies of Hewson and d'Ornano were wrapped in blankets and were buried in a shared grave on the roadside near the town. The troops paraded and Major Clayton read the funeral service. An inscribed cross was made from the wood of a petrol box.

As the patrols left Murzuk they were concealed by a dust storm that blew in from the north and the enemy made no attempt at pursuit. The next day the force captured two Carabinieri (Italian police) on camels, who had come from the small town of Traghen, 50 kilometres east of Murzuk. The town was surrounded and an Italian prisoner was sent in to demand the fort's surrender. About fifteen minutes later a strange procession appeared out of the gates. It was the town headman and elders, leading fifty occupants carrying banners and beating drums, followed by the Italians who laid down their arms. The town was being surrendered in the traditional Fezzan manner. Afterwards, the patrols went on to forts at Umm el Araneb and Gatrun, but the occupants had been forewarned and were prepared, so after some light skirmishing, they were bypassed.

On 14 January, Clayton ended his operations in the Fezzan and took his patrols over rough and broken country southwards to Tummo by a route that had been considered impassable to vehicles. After halting for a day, they travelled to the forward FFL post of Zouar on the south-west slopes of the Tibesti Mountains in Chad. There they rested for several days.

Colonel Bagnold had received orders for the LRDG to co-operate with the FFL forces in Chad in an attack on the Italian-held town of Kufra. Clayton's patrols were put under temporary French command led by Colonel P.F. Leclerc. They left Zouar on 21 January and travelled over some very difficult country to Faya, on to Ounianga, then Sarra, where G Patrol stayed in reserve while Clayton took T Patrol on to Bishara. They were to act as an advance party for the FFL column of 100 vehicles and to reconnoitre to Uweinat.

On 31 January, when T Patrol was at Bishara, an Italian plane flew overhead making observations but did not attack. The trucks dispersed and took cover among rocks in a large valley surrounded by hills at Jebel Sherif. The aircraft later returned and circled over the area to which it directed a patrol of the Auto-Saharan Company, the enemy equivalent of the LRDG. The Italians attacked from the rear, entering the valley from the southern end. They were a strong force, with four Fiat 634N heavy trucks mounting 20mm Breda guns, led by an SPA AS.37 command vehicle. They were also carrying 7.7mm, 8mm and 12.7mm machine guns.

They opened deadly accurate fire from about 200 metres, setting on fire three out of the eleven T Patrol trucks. However, the outcome could have been worse if not for the brave stand of Corporal F.R. Beech. On his truck *Te Anau*, he stood behind his .303 Vickers machine gun and held the attackers at bay long enough to allow the rest of the patrol to get away. He was hit by an explosive bullet and died beside his burning Chevrolet. Also in the crossfire, the Italian postman Signor Colicchia, captured in Murzuk, was killed. The enemy had to abandon one Fiat 634N truck with radiator damage and lost three men killed and two wounded.

The Italians had only covered one entrance, so Clayton took the remaining eight trucks out of the other. Meanwhile, the machine guns on Trooper R.J. Moore's truck *Te Aroha* also held the enemy at bay for a short time before their truck caught fire and had to be abandoned. Moore and his three crew ran into the hills for cover. The truck *Te Paki* was also hit and burning, but the crew were rescued by other vehicles.

The enemy aircraft had now increased to three and began low-level bomb and strafing attacks. Clayton's Ford, *Te Rangi*, received hits that punctured two tyres, the radiator and the fuel tank. Luckily for Clayton, a bullet deflected off his helmet but he was hit in the arm. With the enemy land forces now quickly approaching, it was decided that further resistance was useless and the men surrendered. Clayton, along with his crew, Lance Corporals W.R Adams and L. Roderick, became the first LRDG prisoners of war.

When the Jebel Sherif battle was over, Trooper R.J. Moore and his crew, Guardsmen J. Easton and A. Winchester and RAOC fitter Private A. Tighe, had been left behind. Despite Moore suffering a metal splinter in his foot and Easton having a bad throat wound, they set out on what was to become a torturous ten-day march. By the end of the 336-kilometre trek, with little water and food, the men were delirious and exhausted. Sadly, not long after his rescue, Guardsman J. Easton succumbed to his severe throat wound. Only Moore was still walking when he was picked up by the FFL. He was later awarded the Distinguished Conduct Medal for his leadership.

The patrols rejoined Colonel Leclerc on 1 February, when it was decided that because the Italians at Kufra were now alerted, and in light of T Patrol's losses, to release the LRDG from further service with the French, though one T Patrol truck would remain to assist the FFL with navigation. It later guided them through the desert for their successful attack on Kufra.

Returning to Cairo in early February 1941, the patrols had covered 7,200 kilometres with the loss of four trucks to enemy action and two to mechanical failure. The casualties included three dead, several wounded and three captured. Major Clayton was subsequently awarded the Distinguished Service Order. This early offensive operation provided valuable lessons and prepared the ground for the many future missions the Group was to undertake over the next two years.

Captain P.A. Clayton. Promoted to major in December 1940, he commanded a column of twenty-four vehicles carrying seventy-six men of the New Zealand T1 Patrol and the British Guards, G Patrol. Their mission was an operation against the Italians in the Fezzan region of southern Libya.

Major Clayton with his Ford V8 command car in front. He heads his column of twenty-four vehicles carrying seventy-six men of G and T Patrols on the Fezzan operations.

The two Ford 01 V8 pilot cars that led the raids into the Fezzan. They both mount .303 Vickers machine guns. To assist in engine cooling, the side front of the bonnets have been cut out and replaced with mesh. The Ford on the left was Major Clayton's car, named *Te Rangi*.

(**Opposite, above**) Lieutenant F.B. Edmundson, the LRDG medical officer, leans against his Ford V8 HQ3. His passenger is Sheikh Abd el Galil, the leader of the Libyan Senussi resistance movement. They travelled with the Guards column led by Captain M.D. Crichton-Stuart. Parked alongside is a G Patrol truck, with a name that appears to read *Duke of Colchester*.

(**Opposite, below**) A Guards patrol truck stuck in the sand. Note the compact, highly-stacked stores carried. On occasion these had to be unloaded to help free the vehicle.

(**Above**) A rare moment when the LRDG men looked like regular soldiers. They are armed with .303 Lee Enfield rifles and carry fabric fifty-round ammunition bandoliers. They pose with a Toubou tribesman and his camel in the Fezzan.

(**Above**) The Guards truck G2 in the foreground was damaged beyond repair. It had broken the connecting rod in its engine and was totally dismantled for spare parts. T Patrol trucks are parked in the background.

(**Opposite**) The medical officer's vehicle deeply stuck in the sand. The wicker medical basket is among other stores being unloaded to lighten the Ford for extraction. It looks as if the rear of the vehicle is going to be raised with the aid of blocks and a jack.

(**Below**) Ford V8 command car *Te Rangi* stuck in the soft sand. The patrol member is well-dressed against the cold. The side view displays the distinctive camouflage pattern of the vehicle.

(**Opposite, above**) Major Clayton meeting at Tummo with the Free French of Chad Province discussing plans. The officer on the left is Lieutenant L.B. Ballantyne, T Patrol commander, and Captain J. Massu in the kepi. Also centre: Major Clayton and navigator/intelligence officer Lieutenant W.B. Kennedy Shaw. On the extreme left, Lieutenant F.B. Edmundson looks on.

(**Opposite, below**) Major Clayton, second right, at Kayugi, north of Tibesti, discusses the Fezzan operations with the Free French officers. Supreme and Shell petrol boxes make useful tables. Left: Lieutenant A. Eggenspiller, Lieutenant Colonel J.C. d'Omano (later killed in action) and Captain J. Massu.

(**Above**) Captain J. Massu poses with T Patrol members and Free French *Indigenes*. Note the stretcher handles on the doctor's Ford in front.

(**Below**) The patrols demonstrate the .303 Vickers with the Free French, with Colonel d'Omano testing the weapon. Major Clayton is in the white shirt. The man on the extreme right is Corporal F.R. Beech, who was later killed in action.

T Patrol members and Free French native troops pose against the truck *Te Aute*.

Left: Corporal A.J. Job, Gunner A.E. Sanders and Trooper I.C. Ferguson. The crew of the Bofors gun truck are behind them. Overalls were common desert wear in the early days. They all carry pistols in Pat.37 webbing. The steel helmets, though often worn in action in the early days, were later generally discarded, being too hot and cumbersome.

T and G Patrols with the Free French halt for a rest while on the Fezzan operations.

Centre: Major Clayton and Lieutenant Kennedy Shaw (intelligence officer) interrogate the Italian Carabinieri after the surrender of Traghen.

(**Opposite, above**) G Patrol trucks stuck in an area of soft sand.

(**Opposite, below**) Italian prisoners captured during the Fezzan operations. Left: the Murzuk postman Signor Colicchia (later killed at Jebel Sherif), an airman taken at the Murzuk airfield and two Carabinieri from Traghen.

(**Above**) The column halted before the attack on the town of Murzuk. The local Italian postman was detained to act as a guide. His bicycle was hooked on the back of the truck of Corporal F.R. Beech, who is standing up, looking down at Major Clayton and the Free French.

(**Opposite, above**) Major Clayton's Ford led the patrols towards Murzuk. While the column is halted, Lance Corporal Roderick is positioned behind the machine gun.

(**Opposite, below**) Trooper I.H. McInnes, T Patrol. He won the Military Medal for his effective 2in mortar-shooting against the Italian fort at Murzuk, setting a tower on fire.

(**Above**) The Murzuk airfield buildings burn in the background as a T Patrol truck leaves the action.

(**Below**) In the attack on Murzuk, Lieutenant Colonel J.C. d'Omano and Sergeant C.D. Hewson, T Patrol, were both killed in action. The patrols and Free French salute their combined grave.

(**Above**) The cross was made from the wood of a flimsy petrol box. It is dated '11th Jan 1941' and marked with the Free French Cross of Lorraine and a New Zealand Army 'Onward' badge.

(**Opposite, above**) Following the Murzuk raid, T Patrol cuts through an attractive palm grove as they turn back eastwards on the road to Traghen.

(**Opposite, below**) Major Clayton (with the side-cap) accepting the surrender of the Italian-occupied town of Traghen in January 1941. The trooper in the middle is wearing Italian leather ammunition pouches. The tribal leaders presented themselves with great ceremony.

(**Opposite, above**) The surrender of Traghen was accompanied by drums and dancing, much to the enjoyment of the patrol members.

(**Opposite, below**) T Patrol truck T5, *Te Paki*, found by the Free French on 9 February 1941. It was burned out following the battle of Jebel Sherif. Lying in front of the vehicle is the body of Signor Colicchia, the Murzuk postman killed in the crossfire.

(**Above**) Two burned-out T Patrol trucks at Jebel Sherif: T10 *Te Anau* in front and T6 *Te Aroha*.

A Free French officer examines the burned-out remains of *Te Anau*. Corporal F.R. Beech was killed while firing his Vickers machine gun at the attacking Italian Sahariana forces. This brave action delayed the enemy, enabling most of the patrol to escape. His body was buried at Jebel Sherif, alongside the Italian postman.

The Italian Sahariana Fiat 634N truck was put out of action by the LRDG return fire at Jebel Sherif, damaging its radiator. Its truck mounted a 20mm Breda gun which was removed and the truck left for later recovery. However, it was found by the Free French who set it on fire.

Trooper W.R. ('Wink') Adams. He was with Major Clayton when their Ford V8 was put out of action by Italian aircraft. Both he and his fellow crew member Lance Corporal L. Roderick were captured by the enemy. They became the first LRDG prisoners of war.

Lance Corporal L. Roderick and Trooper E.F. Gorringe. Roderick was captured with Major Clayton. Note the fighting knife strapped to his leg. For a time before the war he was a lightweight Australasian professional boxer.

Trooper P.L. Garland next to his truck T4 *Taipo*. They escaped the Jebel Sherif action.

ILLUSTRATED—June 14, 1941. No. 16. Vol. III

EVERY WEDNESDAY

ILLUSTRATED 3ᵈ·

MOORE *and* TIGHE
*Ten days desert trek
on three pints of water*
(see page 21)

**INSIDE
THE U.S.
EMBASSY**

Trooper R.J. Moore and Private A. Tighe feature on the cover of the 14 June 1941 issue of the *Illustrated Magazine*. Moore, along with three other crew of the truck *Te Aroha* destroyed at Jebel Sherif, walked for ten days before being rescued. The others in the party were Guardsman J. Easton who later died as a result of a throat wound, plus Guardsman A. Winchester and RAOC fitter Alfred Tighe. Moore received the Distinguished Conduct Medal for his leadership.

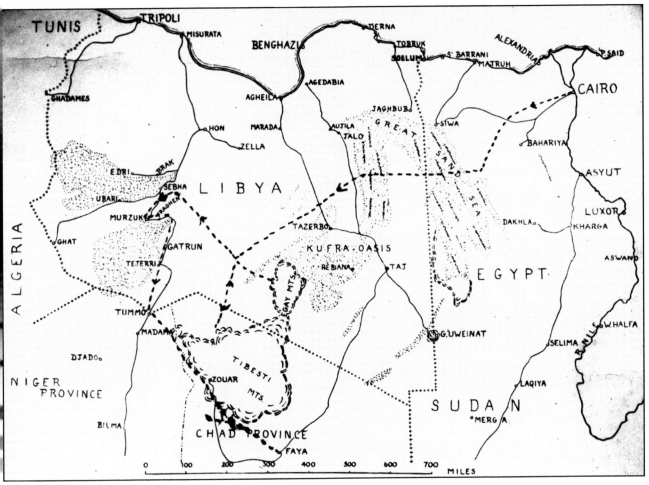

A hand-drawn sketch map that accompanied the 1941 post-operational report of the Fezzan campaign. The arrow lines indicate the route taken. The patrols had covered 7,200 kilometres over all types of desert terrain.

The silver Long Range Patrol (LRP) badge. The dimensions were a 24mm circle and 30mm height including the scroll base. It was created in early 1941 as a commemorative/sweetheart badge to mark the end of the LRP and the beginning of the LRDG when the British Guards joined in December 1940. The scorpion originally had a gold wash, but that easily wore off over time. This example was issued to Sergeant C.D. Hewson, the first LRDG man to be killed in action.

Chapter Three

1941–42: An Overview –
The CMP Ford F30

After about nine months, the well-worn and high-mileage Chevrolet WB 30cwt trucks were replaced by the Canadian Military Pattern (CMP) Ford V8 F30 4 × 4 30cwts. The radiator grilles and vehicle bonnets were removed to assist with cooling and to enable ready access to the radiator and engine. Being four-wheel drive, they were much heavier than the Chevrolet WB and used twice as much fuel, thus drastically reducing the effective range of a patrol. Therefore quartermasters had to take special account of supplies required for a trip in order that additional petrol could be carried. Water and rations had to be carefully calculated in relation to the proposed distance of travel. Consequently, the vehicles became overloaded, which resulted in tyres blowing more often, requiring extra spares to be carried. It also meant, depending on the mission, that the Heavy Section had to establish more forward fuel dumps to accommodate the F30s.

The Ford's four-wheel drive was handy at times, but the truck was prone to overheating which led to greater water consumption. They were also slower than the Chevrolets, which were considered the better vehicle for desert work. Moreover, the Fords were not as popular with the drivers because the V8 motor was mounted between themselves and the front passenger, so it could get very hot, plus was awkward to work on in a hurry. Sergeant R.W.N. Lewis of T1 Patrol wrote in his diary of the problems they were having with their new trucks while on a trip to Kufra:

> 16/04/1941: The V8 Fords are giving a lot of trouble. By the second day four of the batteries had gone flat and there was trouble with some of the gearboxes. The trucks are sticking a lot and having various mechanical problems. Besides the batteries, tie-rods are bending and one steering box has broken. But they certainly get a thrashing, loaded to top capacity and driven over all different types of going.

The Ford 01 V8 15cwt command cars also now needed replacement and were returned to HQ for base transport. Further vehicles were obtained in December 1941 with the issue of twenty-five Chevrolet 1311X3 4 × 2 15cwts. These were useful utility vehicles and were employed as both command and general-purpose light transport. Also a further addition to the fleet was a small number of short-wheel-based Ford F8 8cwts adopted as command cars. These were used for only a few months until July 1942, when the Willys MB 5cwt jeeps were being issued as the standard pilot vehicles.

By late 1941, the LRDG strength had peaked at about 350 personnel and patrol sizes were now split into ten half-patrols, with each having eighteen to twenty men in five or six vehicles. The designations were changed to G1, G2, R1, R2, S1, S2, T1, T2, Y1 and Y2. W Patrol was disbanded. The New Zealand patrols comprised A Squadron, while the British and Rhodesians became B Squadron. Each patrol incorporated specialists: a navigator, radio operator, medical orderly and a vehicle mechanic (fitter), each of whom manned a truck equipped for their role, plus a command or pilot vehicle.

Each vehicle usually carried a crew of three: the truck commander, a driver and a gunner, who may have also been a cook or medical orderly. The truck commander was responsible for the packing of the interior of the truck, including knowing the contents and the placement of every case and reporting the quantities on board to the patrol leader. He also had to maintain a constant lookout for enemy aircraft and ground forces, and to keep station and pass on movement orders to the driver. Furthermore he was responsible for the tactical handling and extraction of his vehicle if it became stuck.

The driver was responsible for the whole of his truck, except the interior of the body and for all the tools and fittings, apart from armament. He had to keep his truck mobile at all times by ensuring regular maintenance, such as checking the oil, water and tyre pressures. With the heavy loads, tyre pressure checks were very important and conducted at every halt. Air was provided by a hose attached to an automatic air pump run from the vehicle's engine. The drivers also had to be alert to the avoidance of hitting rocks and getting stuck in the sand. The selection of the actual track lay directly with him, but the patrol commander was primarily responsible for maintaining the correct speed and direction.

The gunner was not only responsible for the care and maintenance of all armament and munitions, but also to be available to assist with any other general duties as directed by the commander. Every patrol member was trained to be a competent gunner, including the medical orderlies. All the crew were expected to be able to take over each other's responsibilities if required.

In December 1941, the Indian Long Range Squadron (ILRS) was formed. It was led by British officers and senior NCOs. There were also three Indian officers and eighty-two Indian other ranks. The ILRS included an HQ unit and two patrols, with thirty-five vehicles similar to those of the LRDG. They came under the command of the Group in October 1942.

The patrols became masters of behind-the-lines desert operations and in addition to their normal reconnaissance work they developed a more aggressive role. Their vehicles mounted a variety of heavy and light machine guns and the Ford F30s continued to carry the 37mm Bofors anti-tank gun. Using 'hit and run' tactics, they would ambush Axis road convoys, roadhouses, supply dumps, airfields, attack any targets of opportunity and then melt away into the desert. They referred to these actions as 'beat ups'. The LRDG came and went so quickly that the Italians called them 'Pattuglia Fanatasma' (Ghost Patrols), because they never knew where or when these raiders were going to strike next. This caused the Axis forces so much concern that they were forced to withdraw badly-needed troops, armour and aircraft from the front lines to protect their rear areas. Part of their success was being such a small force that could easily conceal itself behind enemy lines in the shadows of dunes and wadis, or widely disperse to become difficult to find.

Appropriately, the insignia chosen for the LRDG was a scorpion within a wheel. Their role was like that of a scorpion, which was a potent symbol of power in a small unit: hiding, watching and waiting, capable of striking suddenly and with deadly effect. The sting in its tail was its firepower combined with the element of surprise.

By late 1941, they were working alongside the Special Air Service (SAS) transporting them to and from their objectives, which were mainly Axis airfields, where by stealth, time-bombs were set and many aircraft destroyed. The LRDG would pick up the raiders and take them home again, sometimes with loss to themselves, while trying to avoid enraged pursuers from the ground and the air. An example of when this partnership had serious consequences for the Group was in December 1941, when T2 Patrol under Lieutenant C.S. Morris was transporting SAS members home after successful raids on Axis airfields.

An Me 110 fighter-bomber had followed the tyre tracks from a recently-raided airfield at Nofilia near Agedabia. Despite intensive anti-aircraft fire from the trucks, it strafed the patrol from a height of about 60ft, killing an SAS officer, Lieutenant T.J. Lewes. Soon after, Ju 87 Stukas assisted by a Fieseler Storch spotter plane appeared and began low-level bombing and strafing attacks that lasted for six hours. Though T2 was now widely dispersed and its vehicles camouflaged, four out of the five Ford F30s were destroyed. The aircraft continued to attack the men on the ground, machine-gunning every bush or mound that might provide cover. The survival of the one truck (T10) was due largely to the courage of Private C.A. Dornbush who, although wounded and his truck hit several times, remained behind his machine gun throughout most of the battle. He was awarded the Military Medal for his action.

Following the attack, Lieutenant Morris could not locate the scattered crews of the destroyed vehicles. So with five T2 and four SAS men, he made the 320-kilometre journey back to base at Jalo in the one surviving truck. Amazingly, the remaining men had survived the air attack, but suffered an exhausting eight-day desert trek before rescue. Eventually the SAS acquired its own jeep transport and operated independently.

In the meantime, a lesser-known and not as exciting task was the imperative survey work being undertaken quietly behind the lines. In 1941, the Group's Survey Section was formed under the command of Captain K.H. Lazarus (Royal Engineers), a New Zealand-born surveyor who had worked in Rhodesia before the war. This work was considered necessary due to the absence of reliable maps of the inner desert regions, large slices of which were completely uncharted, and Italian maps were extremely unreliable. Various major depressions and large wadis were sometimes not indicated and 'roads' (tracks) were often shown many kilometres out of position.

The Survey Section's role was to reconnoitre and survey uncharted areas of the Libyan desert that were likely to assume strategic value. Two or three trucks were used for this work, one being fitted with two sun compasses, one for the driver and one for the use of the surveyor. They divided the desert into different topographical areas and each land type was described and delineated. The positions of oases and other man-made or natural features were also fixed. This task entailed travelling thousands of kilometres behind the lines and was done without the surveyors ever being disturbed by the enemy. The LRDG Air Section Waco aircraft flew contact and resupply missions to maintain the small mapping party. Valuable charts were produced that proved essential for the Eighth Army's future operational planning. At the base of the maps were printed the words 'Surveyed by the LRDG'.

The LRDG was never short of recruits and many men dropped rank so that they could join. For example, in December 1940, Bagnold asked Lieutenant General Bernard Freyberg, C-in-C NZ Division, for further volunteers. Of the 800 men who applied only forty were required, so the Group was always in a position to choose the best. The appeal was the almost complete freedom from drill, guards and fatigues, plus the best army food in the Middle East. It was interesting and often exciting work, with the opportunity to prove oneself without the usual regimental constraints. If an individual showed a particular aptitude for the work, there was a good chance of promotion. For example, a number of men who had joined as privates finished their service with the Group as senior NCOs or officers.

On the debit side there was the strain of operating for long periods behind enemy lines with very little leave, suffering the climatic extremes of heat and cold, sandstorms, thirst, anxiety, malaria and desert sores. In addition, if sick or wounded, captured or lost, there was little chance of assistance apart from what could be provided from their own resources. They had to be resilient, both mentally and physically, and have the wherewithal to survive.

With the loss of transport due to enemy action, or more rarely through serious mechanical failure, it then became a matter of survival. LRDG annals record a number of occasions when men had trekked great distances, up to ten days, sick or wounded, with very little water or rations and had successfully navigated their way to safety. Despite the concerns and hardships of desert life, the men displayed their usual tenacity and stoically got on with the job. The determination and success of this small force was reflected in the fact that a significant number of its members won decorations.

Special Forces soldiers are by their nature unconventional, and it was this quality that characterized most of the soldiers of the LRDG. Many were not regulars but civilians in uniform; because of this they felt they were not bound by 'Regulations' (in their eyes anyway). Even the commanders were chiefly temporary soldiers: business-men, lawyers and farmers who looked at tactical situations with fresh eyes. For example, one of the great LRDG commanders, Lieutenant Colonel Jake Easonsmith, was a wine merchant before the war!

In the field most of the men were highly-disciplined because they appreciated that without self-discipline they could let down or endanger their comrades. They fully understood the team concept. Most had played rugby or other team sports, and providing the officers gave them a fair deal, they would gain respect in return. The patrols (especially the New Zealanders and Rhodesians) often reflected this mutual trust or fellowship, with the officers and men at times addressing each other by their first names. The dangerous nature of LRDG operations, along with the high quality of its personnel, meant that a good level of esprit de corps always prevailed. Those who didn't fit in were soon returned to their units.

Canadian CMP Ford F30 4 x 4 30cwt trucks, newly-issued in Cairo to the Rhodesian S Patrol, March 1941. They have yet to be painted in desert colours and the bonnets and grilles had to be removed to assist engine cooling before they were ready for action.

The CMP Ford F30 4 × 4 30cwt truck, T11, *Te Anau*. In March 1941, due to the high mileage and wear and tear accrued during the Fezzan operations, seventy Ford F30s replaced the original Chevrolets.

Ford F30s lined up outside the Citadel in Cairo before their first trip. The canopy frames were retained for a time, but were eventually discarded.

A good view of new Ford F30s showing weapons and equipment. The vehicle in the foreground is a Bofors gun truck. At the rear, canopy frames appear useful for airing clothing.

A campsite at Tazerbo set up against a Ford F30. Troopers left: H.H. Cleaver and F.W. Jopling.

A Ford F30 collapsed in a well. To assist in cooling the V8 engine, the grille and bonnet were removed. These vehicles were not popular with the drivers because the cab was over the engine. This generated heat that could cause an added discomfort to the driver and passenger.

This F30 drove over a small sand dune at speed and collapsed its front suspension.

The damaged R Patrol truck R7 being towed away.

Trooper B.C. Springford, Y Patrol, stands in front of his Ford F30 *Tipperary Tim*, 1941.

The remains of a direct hit on a Ford F30 truck following a Ju 87 Stuka attack.

Cairo studio photo, December 1941, taken directly following their return after T2 Patrol was shot up by enemy aircraft while working with the SAS. They had lost four out of their five F30 trucks. The men still wear their winter patrol dress. Left: Lance Corporal A.H.C. Nutt, Lieutenant C.S. Morris and Trooper I.G. McCulloch.

An R Patrol F30 *Rotomahana* drives past an overturned Free French Lysander aircraft.

T Patrol fitter Trooper R.T. Porter working on the V8 engine of the F30, with the radiator removed. Four-wheel-drive vehicles were heavy and used more fuel than the two-wheel-drive Chevrolets, which limited their patrol range.

(**Above**) Private L. Payne in front of his truck shelter. The pith helmet was common wear in the early days, but after time usually got knocked about and was eventually discarded. Note the white-painted 2-gallon water cans.

(**Opposite, above**) A Bofors 37mm anti-tank gun mounted in a Ford F30. Though the weapon was fitted to defend against armoured vehicles, it was mainly used against Italian forts and emplacements.

(**Opposite, below**) Citadel in Cairo, 1941. Left to right: General Claude Auchinleck, C-in-C Middle East; Captain Bruce Ballantyne, Commander T Patrol; and Lieutenant Colonel Ralph Bagnold, Commander, LRDG. They inspect a truck-mounted Bofors gun; note the distinctive muzzle brake.

L4406119

Ford F30 T11 side view showing its storage boxes and weapons. It mounts a .303 Vickers heavy machine gun and .55 Boys anti-tank rifle. Note the unusual placement of the spare tyre.

T Patrol F30s towing an Italian Spa AS37 4 × 4 light truck. These were evaluated for a time for possible use by the LRDG but were not adopted. They had been captured from the Auto-Saharan Company.

Y Patrol members test a Spa AS37 down a dune. Left: Trooper A.H. Cave and Trooper H.C. Chard (third man unidentified).

A burned-out F30 following an air attack. Due to the large amount of fuel and munitions carried, LRDG vehicles were always vulnerable to destruction by fire. See the remains of the .303 rifle.

The patrols pass through a gap in 'the Wire'. Built by the Italians, this tangled barbed-wire fence ran 320 kilometres from Bardia to Giarabub, designed to keep the Libyan population from crossing into Egypt.

A captured Italian fuel dump with an F30 in the background.

Heavy Section crew enjoying a meal. Note the great variation in dress and headwear. The man in the centre looks like he is wearing an Italian tunic. Dress Regulations did not exist while the LRDG were out on patrol. Right: Second Lieutenant A. Denniff. He wears a greatcoat over his sheepskin coat, indicating very cold weather.

(**Opposite, above**) Approaching Wadi Sora, open landscape with mountains casting shadows in the distance. Such shaded areas provided excellent camouflage environments for the patrols.

(**Opposite, below**) An LRDG column well spread out after a halt. This enabled the patrol to widely disperse in case of air attack, making them less of a target.

(**Above**) A comfortable shelter erected against a Ford F30. Lieutenant S.W. Ellingham rests among the clutter of stores and equipment, which indicates more than an overnight camp. The Shell fuel boxes make useful furniture. The bandage on his knee covers a desert sore, a common affliction on a long patrol.

T Patrol camp at Kufra. A Ford F30 canopy frame employed as an effective shelter. The man at the rear with a bandage is Private R.O. Spotswood; the one in front is not identified.

Private R.O. Spotswood and (right) Trooper I.G. McCulloch relax. Not a tidy camp, with a broken petrol box, beer bottle and helmet lying in the sand.

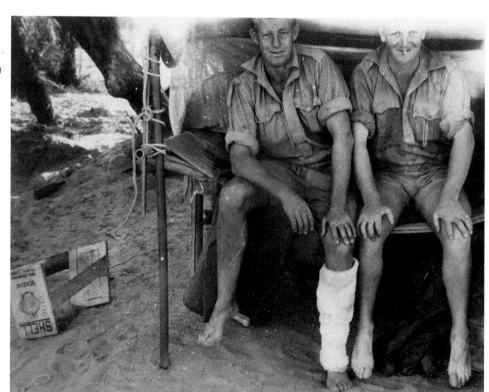

A patrol setting up camp. A well in the foreground is inspected, while a truck on the left is being serviced under the shade of a canopy. The broken wooden Shell boxes were used to make cooking fires.

R Patrol members enjoying a meal served from the back of an F30. Note the variety of dress worn.

(**Above**) A steep slope being negotiated by a Y Patrol F30. As a four-wheel-drive vehicle, care had to be taken not to crack the two differential housings against large rocks.

(**Opposite, above**) Rhodesian S Patrol camp at Zighen. Despite its harsh surroundings, the men had established a reasonably comfortable base built around a cluster of palm trees. They called it 'The Rhodesia Club'. An F30 is parked in the foreground, while in the distance the lone palm acted as a lookout point.

(**Opposite, below**) Damaged after crashing over a dune, the Ford V8 *Te Rangi II* had to be returned to the Citadel workshops in Cairo in the back of a Ford F30 truck. Trooper W.D. Burnand stands alongside.

By 1941, the LRDG had adopted the Arab headdress or *keffiyeh* as their formal dress, and for optional wear in the field. T Patrol officers left: Lieutenant E.W. Ellingham and Captain L.B. Ballantyne pose on parade with their Sam Browne harness. This was not normally worn in the field, usually replaced by the Pat.37 web holster and belt.

The same two officers, Ellingham and Ballantyne, in more informal patrol dress.

(**Left**) A studio photo of Private C.B. McKenzie. He displays his LRDG shoulder titles and brass LRDG scorpion badge on the black *agal* of his *keffiyeh*. The headdress worn in the desert was good protection from the sun, wind, dust and flies. It could also be used as a dirty water filter or as a small shade cover, as the Arabs did using sticks.

(**Below**) The official LRDG cast brass cap badge, a scorpion in a wheel. The original design was to have a crown on top, but the final issue excluded it. The actual diameter is 33mm.

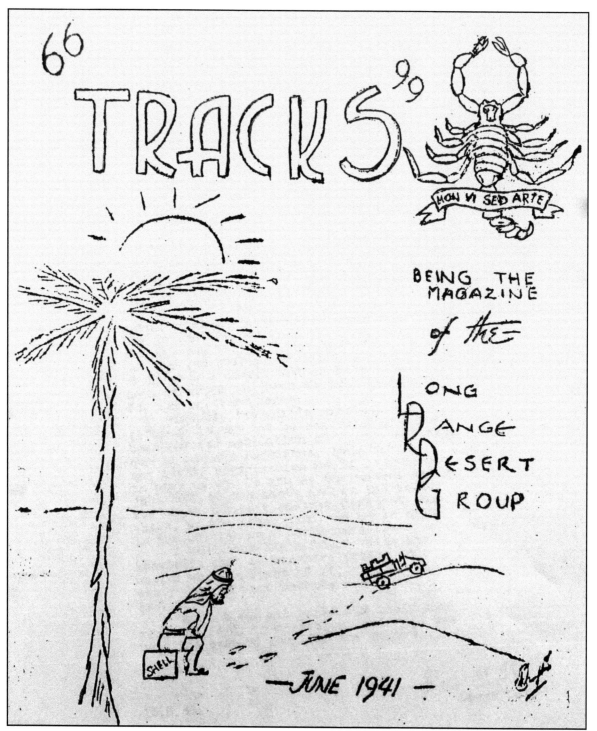

The cover of the LRDG magazine *Tracks*, June 1941 issue. These were simply bound like a pamphlet. It provided some light reading and news for the troops. Note the motto on the scorpion: *Non Vi Sed Arte*, Latin for 'Not by Strength, by Guile'.

(**Above, left**) Gunner E. ('Sandy') Sanders, T Patrol, dressed in typical LRDG summer dress. He wears the RTR Pat. open-top web holster. He served on both the Bofors and Breda gun trucks. In 1942, using his Breda gun, Sanders won the Military Medal by knocking out four German vehicles pursuing his patrol.

(**Above, right**) Captain K.H. Lazarus led the LRDG Survey Section. Their role was to reconnoitre and survey uncharted areas of the Libyan desert that were likely to assume strategic value. They produced valuable charts that proved essential for the Eighth Army's future operational planning. Note the LRDG-issued leather sandals (*chapplies*). Later Lazarus also commanded fighting patrols and served with distinction in the Dodecanese operations of 1943.

T Patrol December 1941. Left: Trooper R.F. White, Trooper W.G. Gerrard and Second Lieutenant P. Freyberg, the son of General Freyberg, C-in-C New Zealand Forces. He was attached to the LRDG to gain field experience, though he was later wounded when the patrol came under air attack.

(**Above, left**) The .303 Lewis gun was the standard light machine gun used by the patrols. However, by mid-1942 they were generally replaced by Vickers K machine guns. Gunner T.E. Walsh employs his Lewis in an anti-aircraft role. (**Above, right**) Sergeant R.W.N. Lewis sights his Lewis gun mounted on his truck. The exposed base of the forty-seven-round magazine could allow dust to cause a jam. The weapons were usually covered until required for action. Note the sun compass on the dashboard.

Signalman T. Scriven, attached to T2 Patrol. Most of the signallers in the patrols came from the Royal Corps of Signals. The No. 11 (HP) radio was operated in the Ford F30 in the manner shown. These were robust and reliable sets and used throughout the desert campaign.

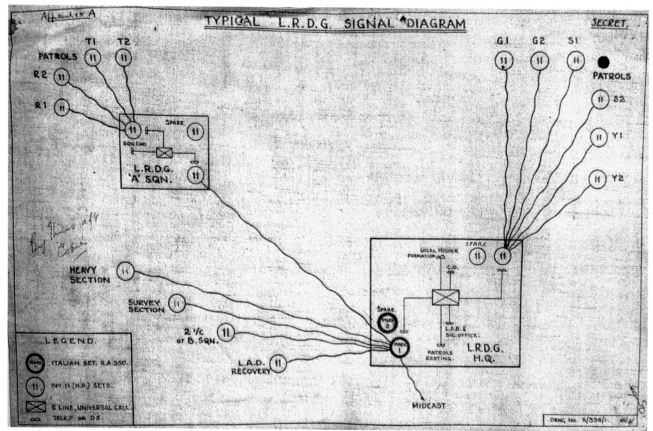

Wartime LRDG signal diagram. With the primary function of the Group being intelligence-gathering, successful and efficient signalling was essential to the achievement of a mission.

Y Patrol F30 radio truck. Left: Trooper L.S. Coombs and Signalman K.L. Barbour. Note the vehicle is partly camouflaged with scrub.

General Claude Auchinleck, accompanied by Captain L.B. Ballantyne, views LRDG troops during an inspection in the Citadel in Cairo. Parading in formal dress was a rare occasion for the men.

Modified for desert work, a short-wheel-based Ford F8 2 × 4 named T1, *Te Rangi III*. These were used for a limited time as command cars. The driver is Trooper W.D. Burnand. It mounts a covered .303 heavy Vickers machine gun.

Another view of the Ford F8, with Captain L.B. Ballantyne in front and Trooper Burnand next to a .303 Vickers K machine gun. These vehicles were often referred to as 'the baby Fords'.

Captain Ballantyne next to his Ford F8 command vehicle. It was nicknamed 'Stinker'.

Y Patrol Ford F8 *D'Artagnan* stuck in the sand.

Chapter Four

1942–43: An Overview – Chevrolet 1533X2 4 × 2 30cwt

In March 1942, to replace the Ford F30s, a consignment of specially-ordered and adapted Canadian Chevrolet 1533X2 4 × 2 trucks had arrived. Though they were only two-wheel drive, an extra low ratio of gears with a six-cylinder engine producing lower fuel consumption made them ideal for desert work. The American Willys jeep, which was being used by the SAS, was also adopted by the LRDG as their command or pilot vehicle. The patrols now operated as four to five trucks, depending on the mission, led by the commander's jeep.

With the new Chevrolets, they progressed to mounting heavier armament with greater fire-power, which increased their offensive capability. They progressed through a whole variety of machine guns. Initially they continued with the .303 Lewis and water-cooled Vickers, and then used whatever they could find from crashed aircraft, wrecked vehicles or taken from the enemy. For example, single and twin .303 aircraft Browning machine guns, fitted with mountings made in their workshops, also adopting tank Besa machine guns or Italian Breda 12.7mm machine guns. The Boyes .55 anti-tank rifles, carried since the beginning, were now removed as they were of little use. Armoured vehicles were rarely encountered by the LRDG and, if so, avoided as quickly as possible.

After a time, the Lewis guns were replaced with the .303 Vickers K; fed by a 100-round flat pan magazine, they proved very effective, especially when mounted as a dual combination. Originally designed as RAF air gunners' weapons, they were favoured by both the LRDG and SAS for their reliability and fire-power. Heavier calibre weapons were now also being acquired. Initially the water-cooled .50 Vickers heavy machine gun, then later the lighter .50 Brownings, both Air Pattern and HB models, became the standard.

Also with the new trucks, the cumbersome heavy Bofors gun was discarded and replaced by the more versatile Italian semi-automatic 20mm Breda Model 35 gun. This was mounted on a carriage turntable, bolted through the rear deck onto the truck chassis. Operated by a crew of two, they fired a twelve-round clip and proved to be a very effective and dependable weapon. One was attached to each patrol.

By 1942/43, the truck-mounted weapons could prove devastating against concentrated enemy targets such as convoys or parked aircraft. One account recorded in Kennedy Shaw's *Long Range Desert Group* (1945), described the effect of the mixed armaments used in an attack by Captain J.A.L Timpson's G1 Patrol:

> Driving with the headlights on we came to the Road House, and passing by slowly, opened up on men and vehicles. The blaze of fire was tremendous, the first three trucks firing with one Breda 12.7 (tracer, incendiary, A.P. and H.E.) two Vickers .303, three Vickers K, one twin Browning, one single Browning and a Lewis. In fact there was too much fire, for the rear trucks were blinded by the light of those ahead and the multi-coloured ricochet of the tracer. Six large trucks were parked by the roadside and into those we poured ammunition.

To take part in the British offensive in Cyrenaica in November 1941, the LRDG was placed under the command of the newly-formed Eighth Army. The whole Group was moved from Kufra to Siwa. The patrols were to watch the desert tracks to the south of Jebel Akhdar and to report on the movements of enemy reinforcements and withdrawals. However, on 24 November when the battle in the Tobruk-Bardia area had reached a critical stage, the role of the LRDG was suddenly changed. They were issued orders for the patrols to 'Act with utmost vigour offensively against any targets or communications within your reach.'

Consequently, Y1 and Y2 Patrols were ordered to patrol and ambush on roads in the Melchili-Derna-Gazala area: G1 and G2 the main road near Agedabia, and the combined Rhodesian and New Zealand patrols S2 and R2 the Benghazi-Barce-Marawa road. Y1 damaged fifteen vehicles in a transport park, Y2 captured a small fort with about twenty prisoners and S2 and R2 ambushed nine vehicles and killed and wounded a number of the enemy. G1 made two independent attacks on road traffic and shot up a few vehicles.

These road convoy raids continued into 1942, which included laying mines and tearing up telephone underground cables or destroying telegraph poles. To enable the patrols to escape without being observed, most of these attacks took place at night. The enemy had little chance to defend themselves against the devastating firepower of the LRDG. Consequently, great apprehension grew in the minds of the Italian drivers, many of whom were semi-civilian contractors, as they feared when their turn might be next. Because these actions were usually unopposed, some patrol members expressed empathy towards their opponents. As Trooper Keith Tippett of T1 Patrol recalled:

> It was absolutely horrifying the way we shot at them, but it had to be done to cause havoc. In the light of the flames of burning trucks you would see men trying to get out of their vehicles, it was quite sickening. Normally we would just

hit and run and didn't linger to view the carnage. We weren't supposed to bring any wounded back, though occasionally some of us did.

Trooper Derek Parker of T1 Patrol also recalled the horror of shooting up convoys:

The poor beggars didn't have much of a show at all, we cut them to pieces. It was a pretty cruel sort of fighting, but when you were way behind the lines, it was either them or us. We always made sure, where we possibly could, that it was them. I always felt a bit guilty and ashamed about some of these raids; the one-sided ambushes seemed a bit unfair.

A large percentage of the information the Eighth Army received about enemy movements came via the radios of the LRDG stationed behind the lines. Their most significant intelligence-gathering role was the 'Road Watch' – constant observation, day and night, of the Tripoli-Benghazi road (Via Balbia), 643 kilometres behind enemy lines. It was undertaken between 2 March and 21 July 1942 to assess the enemy's strength in Cyrenaica, where the Middle East HQ was planning an offensive. A well-concealed patrol would provide a roster of two men, hidden close to the road, in twenty-four-hour shifts. They recorded every sighting of enemy armour, supplies and troops travelling to and from the front line. It took three patrols to do this work; while one was watching the road for a week to ten days, the other was going out from the base at Siwa to relieve it. Meanwhile, the third was making the long journey back. Both squadrons shared in this important though sometimes tiresome task.

As Ron Landon-Lane of R Patrol recalled: 'You look at your watch at 11, and look again about four hours later and it is 11.15! Of all the patrol duties, this was the most hated, yet one of the most important!' The LRDG Intelligence officer Bill Kennedy Shaw wrote that he considered that it was the most useful job the LRDG ever did and wished Rommel could have read about it! What best sums up the value of the Road Watch is in an analysis written by the Director of Military Intelligence at GHO in Cairo in late 1942:

The LRDG Road Watch provided the only trained traffic observers. Not only is the standard of accuracy and observation exceptionally high, but the patrols are familiar with the most recent illustrations of enemy vehicles and weapons. During periods of withdrawal of reinforcements of the enemy, the LRDG had provided an indispensable basis of certain facts on which calculations of enemy strength can be based. Without their reports we would frequently have been in doubt as to the enemy's intentions, when knowledge of them was all important; and our estimate of enemy strength would have been far less accurate and accepted with less confidence.

The Road Watch immediately in the rear of the El Aghelia position has been of quite exceptional importance and the information which it provided, in spite of interruptions due to a difficult and dangerous situation, had been invaluable. From the point of view of military intelligence the risks and casualties which the patrols have accepted and are accepting have been more than justified.

The success of the LRDG's behind-the-lines intelligence-gathering role, compared to the risk, did not go without comment from one of its members. Trooper F.W. Jopling wrote in his diary:

I can truly say that it is a miracle the LRDG gets away with it, the way we have up till now. If GHQ wants information, they send us off to do the job, whereupon we set out in unarmoured and practically unarmed trucks, against armoured cars or planes, which are the two most likely things we would strike, and bring back the information required or prisoners who can give it, and generally a lot more besides. It seems to me the LRDG is doing the impossible and getting away with it.

As masters of desert travel and navigation, the LRDG was often asked to guide others to their objectives. These included units such as the SAS, the Libyan Arab Force, the Free French, the Sudan Defence Force and various Commando teams. Furthermore, they undertook other tasks such as inserting, supplying and collecting British and Arab undercover agents, recovering downed air crew and rescuing Allied prisoners of war. The Group referred to this activity as the 'Libyan Taxi Service'. Between December 1940 and April 1943, there were only fifteen days on which a patrol was not operating behind or on the flanks of the enemy. The unit had lived up to its unofficial motto, as penned by Dr F.B. Edmundson, New Zealand Medical Corps and LRDG medical officer: 'Not by strength, by guile.'

In 1942 the LRDG ordered a consignment of 200 specially-built Canadian Chevrolet 1533X2 4 × 2 30cwt trucks. They were prepared and outfitted for desert work. This one is being marked as a T Patrol vehicle. Note the size of the metal sand tray and the brand-new spare desert sand tyre in the rear. These replaced the CMP F30s.

(**Opposite, above**) T Patrol Chevrolet T8 *Te Taniwha* at Kufra, with no stores or weapons mounted. These two-wheel-drive vehicles were ideal for desert work and much preferred because of extra low-ratio gears and a six-cylinder engine that consumed less fuel.

(**Above**) A new radio truck T9, *Te Aroha III*. Driver Private T.E. Ritchie; right, Trooper F.W. Jopling; Signalman T. Scriven standing. Note the painted Kiwi on the bonnet indicating a T Patrol vehicle. Stacked on the left are the Wyndom aerial poles that when erected and employed could achieve transmissions over great distances.

(**Opposite, below**) T1 Patrol men listen to the news and music on their Phillips receiver mounted on the radio truck, alongside the No. 11 set. Note the camouflage net covering the vehicle.

(**Opposite, above**) To replace the cumbersome, heavy 37mm Bofors gun, Italian 20mm Breda Model 35 guns were mounted on the new Chevrolets. They proved to be very effective and reliable weapons. One was attached to each patrol. This is the Rhodesian S Patrol truck S6.

(**Opposite, below**) Breda gun, side view, Kufra 1942. Gun crew, left to right: Private C.A. Dornbush, Trooper A.G. Ferguson and Trooper K. Kelly. The 20mm cannon was a dual-purpose weapon intended to be used against both aircraft and vehicles.

(**Above**) T2 Patrol Breda gun truck T10 and crew. Left to right: Trooper I.G. McCulloch, Trooper A.G. Ferguson, Private C.A. Dornbush, Private C.B. McKenzie and Trooper M.V. Stewart.

R Patrol Breda gun truck R7, travelling in an open plain.

A meal being prepared by Sergeant R.W.N. Lewis in the rear of a T Patrol Breda truck. A Libyan servant named Hamed looks on. The rear drop-down tray provides a useful table.

Private C.B. McKenzie undertakes engine maintenance on Breda gun truck T10. Note the spare truck spring in the sand mat cradle.

Trooper A.P. Renwick of R Patrol stands beside his Breda truck. The gun fired twelve-round clips, so the 20mm rounds would have been removed from the links before use.

T1 Patrol column leaving Siwa. The leading truck *Tutira III* mounts a .50 calibre water-cooled Vickers heavy machine gun.

The Chevrolet 1311X3 15cwt medical inspection vehicle has met G Patrol to receive Guardsman E. Murray, who was wounded in an air attack at Fuka on 15 July 1942. His commander Lieutenant R.B. Gurdon was mortally wounded. The medical vehicle had a purpose-built canopy to protect patients from the heat and flies.

Rhodesian S Patrol truck *Louise* mounting a .303 Vickers machine gun heads out on a desert mission. The officer is Second Lieutenant J.R. Olivey. He won the Military Cross in an action with his patrol, destroying an enemy convoy. Olivey went on to serve with great distinction in the Dodecanese operations on Levitha and Leros, where he won a bar to his MC and was made a prisoner of war.

An imposing front view of the Y Patrol Chevrolet Y11 *Chattanooga Choo Choo*. At this time Y Patrol vehicles featured the distinctive scorpion symbol. Note the heavy towing chain attached to the bumper.

(**Above**) A camp site shelter rigged between two T Patrol trucks.

(**Below**) R Patrol truck R4 stuck deep into the sand. A trench had to be dug first before placing the sand trays for extraction. Note the heavy load stowed in the vehicle.

(**Opposite, above**) A rare occurrence: heavy rain in the desert which caused flooding. This R Patrol truck is being towed out after becoming bogged in the wet sand.

(**Opposite, below**) A common desert travel event. Negotiating sharp rocks and stones often caused punctures or ripped tyres. Changing the heavy 10in sand tyre wheel was hard work. The wide tread was necessary over the softer desert terrains, where sometimes the tyre was also partially deflated for better traction.

Stuck on the crest of a dune. It could be a difficult extraction, with the belly of the heavily-loaded vehicle resting on the sand ridge.

A 10-ton White truck HS5 of the Heavy Section. These were essential in keeping the forward LRDG supply dumps provisioned. The crew are resting under the vehicle in the heat of the day.

Front view of the Heavy Section Mack NR 9 10-ton truck. Note the large condenser fitted by the door to recycle the water from the radiator. Trooper N.R. Campbell stands alongside as a comparison to the height of the vehicle.

(**Opposite, above**) R Patrol enjoying a Christmas meal. Note the variety of dress and headgear worn, reflecting the cooler winter season.

(**Opposite, below**) A gazelle head mounted on the front of a T Patrol truck. The rest of the animal would have been a fresh addition to the rations. Note the Kiwi painted on the bonnet, which indicated T Patrol.

(**Above**) The LRDG used to shoot wild animals for sport or for food for the pot. In this case it was a cheetah for sport.

(**Opposite, above**) An animal hangs on the back of this truck, which could be an oryx or a goat. The central mounted weapon is a .50 Vickers heavy machine gun. It had a large wooden shoulder butt used to direct the gun. This truck is unusual in that it has a full windscreen. Most had them removed or were fitted with small aero screens.

(**Opposite, below**) Christmas dinner and beer in the shade of the Zella oasis, 1942.

(**Above**) The patrols often came across some unusual features in the desert. This petrified tree was dubbed 'Penis Rock' by the men. Standing alongside it is Trooper J.T. Bowler, who was later killed in action in the Aegean in 1943.

Bombay

(**Opposite, above**) In December 1941, the LRDG was issued with twenty-five Chevrolet 1311x3 4 × 2 15cwt trucks. Smaller than the 1942 Chevrolets, they made good utility vehicles. Trooper I.G. McCulloch is standing in front.

(**Above**) A 15cwt Chevrolet circles Mushroom Rock.

(**Opposite, below**) A Bristol Bombay transport, Siwa, 4 March 1942. A Chevrolet 15cwt is carrying Lieutenant E.M. Tobin to be evacuated by air. He was suffering from diphtheria and required medical treatment in Cairo.

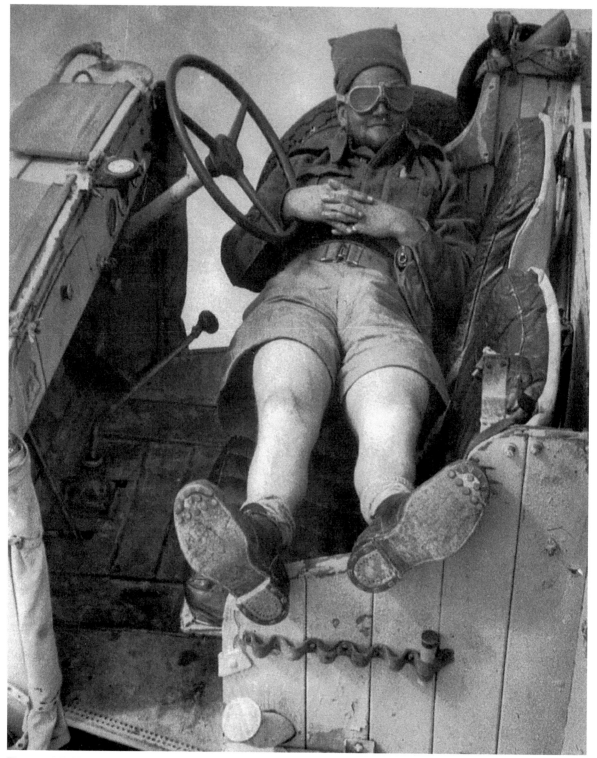

Trooper I.G. McCulloch rests inside his Chevrolet 15cwt. Note the sun compass and the flare cartridge holder on the side panel.

In the foreground a Chevrolet 1311x3 4 × 2 15cwt. Behind is the 1942 Chevrolet T2 *Te Taniwha*. With these vehicles, a number of original grille bars were removed to assist cooling; also to gain easy access to the radiator should holes need to be plugged in an emergency.

A cooling swim for the patrols at the Figure Eight pool at Siwa oasis. A Chevrolet 15cwt is parked behind the pool.

By July 1942, the LRDG acquired Willys MB 5cwt jeeps as command/pilot cars. This example is being examined by patrol members in Kharga, 1942. Like the trucks, the water condenser in the front is used to recycle the water from the radiator. Also part of the jeep grille has been removed to assist cooling and gain easy access to the radiator.

A heavily-loaded jeep waits behind a truck bogged in the sand.

An S Patrol jeep named *Babs*, and *Sebakwe* after a region in Rhodesia. The driver is unidentified.

A heavily-armed column loaded with supplies, led by the commander's jeep on a desert mission. All weapons are covered.

By 1942, as the LRDG's role was becoming more aggressive in attacking enemy convoys and airfields, they were fitting better weapons. This Rhodesian truck S11 mounts specially-adapted twin .303 aircraft Brownings. These, combined with other patrol machine guns, could produce devastating fire-power. Left: Sergeant C.C.B. Ryan, Corporal A.E.F. Bailey and Corporal S.N. Eastwood.

T1 Patrol Signalman W. Morrison behind his .50 Browning Air Pattern machine gun, 1943. These reliable, heavy-calibre weapons proved very useful against enemy transport and aircraft.

Sergeant W.H. Rail behind a .50 Browning M2HB heavy machine gun in 1943. Note the folded stretcher on the side of the truck.

LRDG troopers pose with .50 calibre ammunition belts.

(**Above**) Sergeant W.H. Rail tests a Besa 7.92mm machine gun. These were usually mounted in British armoured vehicles. This example has a crude stock fitted and was likely obtained from a tank wreck. The man on the left is holding a pistol.

(**Opposite, above**) S2 Patrol with their heavily-armed and laden Chevrolets on a desert halt.

(**Opposite, below**) Trooper I.G. McCulloch behind his .303 water-cooled Vickers machine gun.

(**Above**) T1 Patrol, Siwa, 1942. Top left: Signalman T. Scriven (British signaller attached to patrol), Trooper R.E. Hay, Trooper K. Kelly, Trooper S.D. Parker, Trooper H.D. Mackay and Trooper K.E. Tippett. Centre row: Trooper B.F. Shepherd, Lance Corporal A.H.C. Nutt, Corporal R.W.N. Lewis, Captain N.P. Wilder, Corporal M.H. Craw, Private T.E. Ritchie and Trooper F.W. Jopling. Front: Gunner E. Sanders, Trooper T.B. Dobson, Trooper T.A. Milburn, Private J.L.D. Davis and Trooper P.V. Mitford. At this time the patrol took part in a number of ambush actions on the Agedabia-Benghazi road, shooting up enemy convoys. Note the twin .303 aircraft Brownings mounted on the truck.

(**Opposite, above**) The remains of enemy fuel tankers and trailers following an LRDG convoy raid. These vehicles were favoured as easy targets for ambush attacks.

(**Opposite, below**) LRDG behind-the-lines hit-and-run attacks on convoys and roadhouses caused much concern to the enemy as they thought they were safe within their own rear areas. A trooper inspects a burned-out Italian Fiat 626 supply truck.

An Italian SPA TL37 abandoned after a convoy attack.

A trooper sits in a German Marder III tank destroyer found alongside the road.

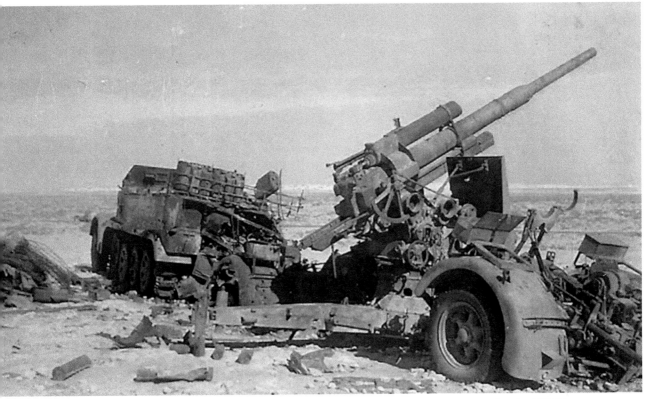

A burned-out Sd.Kfz.7 half-track towing an 88mm anti-aircraft gun. It was not uncommon for the LRDG to come across the debris of previous battles while on missions.

The LRDG were experts at camouflage, as seen with this truck completely concealed while operating the Road Watch behind enemy lines.

The Road Watch was established 8 kilometres from Mussolini's *Arae Philaenorum*, called the Marble Arch by the Allies. This straddled the Tripoli-Benghazi road in Libya, which was kept under observation from March till July 1942. The photo was taken in 1943 with LRDG trucks parked underneath.

R Patrol members after two months behind the lines. Heavily bearded, they looked like 'Bearded Brigands', as one Cairo newspaper described them. From top left: Trooper E.J. Dobson and Trooper A. Boys. Middle: Trooper A.R. Renwick, Trooper L.T. Campbell, Trooper L.A. Ellis, Trooper J.B. Magee, Second Lieutenant R.J. Landon-Lane and Trooper H.L. Mallet (KIA, Levitha, 24 October 1943). Front: Private J.E. Gill, Private R.R. Williams, Trooper F.D. Rhodes and Trooper A.M.D. Stewart.

While on operations, the LRDG often came across downed aircraft and the aftermath of desert battles. Here they are examining a burned-out Italian Ju 87 R-5 of No. 209 Squadron.

A patrol stops to examine a downed Messerschmitt Me 109 fighter. The trooper in the foreground has acquired an RAF sheepskin-lined flying jacket, very warm against the winter cold.

A crash-landed Junkers Ju 88 being explored by the LRDG. Anything useful was recovered, including weapons that if not taken were disabled.

An LRDG trooper poses in front of a crash-landed Italian Savoia-Marchetti SM.82 transport/bomber found in the desert. A mangled body and a grave were discovered alongside this aircraft.

Patrol members examine a crashed Heinkel He 111.

(**Above**) Y Patrol truck *Aramis*. The crew assist with refuelling a Ford Marmon Herrington armoured car at Siwa.

(**Opposite, above**) Occasionally, the LRDG encountered both Axis and Allied armoured cars undertaking forward reconnaissance work. After a desert meeting with T2 Patrol, a King's Dragoon Guards crew pose for a photo alongside their Marmon Herrington armoured car.

(**Opposite, below**) An Afrika Korps Sd.Kfz.223 *Panzerfunkwagen* (radio) armoured car in a dug-in position. The LRDG usually tried to avoid armoured vehicles; however, in January 1943 at Wadi ZemZem, S Patrol encountered two Sd.Kfz.222 armoured cars mounting 20mm guns. The patrol set one on fire with its .50 Browning machine guns, while the other fought back. In the ensuing battle, Gunner E.J. Henderson was killed. This detailed photo came from a captured German camera uplifted by an LRDG trooper.

Lieutenant Colonel David Stirling, founder of the Special Air Service (SAS). On the truck radio is Major Don Steele, Commanding Officer of A(NZ) Squadron, LRDG. These officers organized many successful operations together.

(**Opposite, above**) In the initial SAS operations, the LRDG transported the men to and from their targets, usually airfields. Later they operated independently with their own jeeps. Here unidentified SAS men travel with R2 Patrol members: left, Trooper J.C. Lucas and Trooper M.E. Hammond. Lucas is wearing a captured German cap with a New Zealand 'Onward' badge attached.

(**Opposite, below**) Photo taken in Cairo 1942: T2 Patrol members with the L Detachment, SAS. The men had recently completed a raid on Nofilia airfield together. Back left: Lance Corporal A.H.C. Nutt, Trooper F.S. Brown and Trooper I.G. McCulloch. Front: SAS Sergeant J.E. Almonds and Sergeant E.T. Lilley. They are wearing the first pattern white SAS beret; the colour was later changed to beige.

(**Above**) Colonel John Haselden went behind the lines to spy dressed as an Arab. He was transported and picked up from his operations by the LRDG, in this case by a Ford F30. These incursion drop-off and pick-up missions were dubbed 'The Libyan Taxi Service'.

(**Opposite, above**) The patrols also carried observers on various tasks. November 1942: Captain Alistair Guild's R1 Patrol enjoying a cup of tea. Top left: Signalman Evans, Trooper A. Connelly, Captain M. Pilkington (observer, Arab Legion), Private F.J. Whitaker, Private L.J. Middlebrook and Lance Corporal N. O'Malley. Sitting, left: Second Lieutenant R.J. Landon-Lane, Private R. Rawson, Captain A.L. Guild, Trooper P.G. Reid, Lance Corporal M.D. Richardson and Private M.F. Fogden. A few days after this photo was taken, Captain Pilkington and Lance Corporal O'Malley were killed when the patrol was strafed in an air attack. Private M.F. Fogden was wounded.

(**Opposite, below**) Private M.F. Fogden at the wheel of his truck R2 *Rotowhero*. On 18 November 1942, his patrol was shot up by Italian CR.42 fighters, Fogden was wounded and his vehicle put out of action.

Private Fogden had to suffer a three-day journey in the back of a Breda gun truck to reach a suitable landing ground for a Blenheim bomber to air-lift him out. Members of the Sudan Defence Force look on.

With the glare of the sun and dust while travelling, this image shows typical issue sunglasses and sand goggles being worn. Note the position of the sun compass. Left: Lance Corporal R.A. Ramsay; right, Trooper H.D. Mackay.

Heavily-laden S Patrol trucks gather for a patrol break.

Private A.F. ('Blondie') Goddard of S Patrol poses in front of his truck *Shangani III*, named after a river in Southern Rhodesia. This patrol usually displayed a distinctive scorpion plate on the front of their 1942 Chevrolets.

One of the tasks of the LRDG was also rescuing downed airmen. Here they take care of the injured crew of a crashed USAAF B-24 bomber.

Injured USAAF crew members being treated by an RAF doctor who travelled with the patrol to pick up the Americans. They employ the shelter of the truck for shade.

Chapter Five

The Long Range Desert Group Air Section

Because they could not rely on the RAF to fly LRDG-related missions when and where they wanted to go in the desert, the Group made a decision to acquire their own aircraft. Colonel Bagnold and Major G.L. Prendergast managed to obtain two small American-built Waco biplane cabin aircraft that were on the Egyptian Civil Register. They had been kept in excellent condition by the Egyptian mechanics of an airline company Misr Airways at Cairo's civil airport, with spare parts being obtained direct from the USA.

They were two different models. Waco Model YKC was a four-seater powered by a 225hp seven-cylinder Jacobs L4 engine. The other was a Waco Model ZGC five-seater equipped with a more powerful 285hp seven-cylinder Jacobs L5 engine. They became known to the LRDG as the Little and Big Waco. Neither was radio-equipped and their passenger capacity was reduced when it was realized that each required a navigator as well as the pilot. They had the back seats removed and a fold-up canvas seat put in their place so that they could carry a wounded man and any supplies or equipment that had to be freighted. Also drift sights were fitted to each and the engine cowlings modified to give better cooling. The aircraft were repainted in camouflage and RAF roundels applied. No weapons were installed.

The difference in cruising speeds, 115mph (100 knots) and 140mph (122 knots), made the ability to fly them together difficult. Their range was 300 miles, but by establishing intermediate petrol dumps and taking some risk, Kufra to Cairo could be flown in a day. The Egyptian aircraft company Misr Airways undertook most major servicing requirements, as did occasionally the RAF, whereas regular maintenance was done by the LRDG.

In April 1941 a New Zealander, Trooper R.F.T. Barker, was selected for the LRDG and it was soon discovered that he was a pre-war qualified civilian pilot with 129 hours solo flying time to his credit. He had enlisted in the Royal New Zealand Air Force (RNZAF) in February 1940, but because of his age (35), the RNZAF requested that after his 'wings' training, he remain in New Zealand as an instructor. However, he was determined to go overseas so he managed to obtain a discharge and transferred to the army instead, eventually arriving in the Middle East in December 1940. After being accepted by the Group and his skills ascertained, he was immediately promoted to sergeant pilot and seconded to the newly-created LRDG Air Section. He joined fellow pilot Major Prendergast, who was now Officer Commanding LRDG but also a skilled aviator who explored the desert in the 1930s from the ground and the air.

With all the modifications completed, the aircraft were first received by the LRDG on 13 April 1941, landing at Siwa. They went on to provide much valuable service to the Group, for liaison, reconnaissance, delivering essential supplies, spare parts and mail, plus short-range casualty evacuation, also for in keeping in touch with GHQ in Cairo and the LRDG Survey Section in remote areas behind the lines. On the Little Waco, Sergeant Barker painted below the cockpit window the LRDG initials and just rear of the engine cowling, a small black Kiwi within a shield. Barker was later commissioned and by the end of the war held the rank of captain.

There was no radio or direction-finding equipment carried so to assist when required, two truck navigators had to be trained in aerial work. If they were ever uncertain about their position, they would just land and check their calculations with the aid of a 'sunshot' using a sextant. The Wacos flew great distances above vast wastelands in all conditions, over dust or sandstorms and in desert haze, with their careful navigation bringing them safely to an appointed rendezvous. Being sturdy reliable aircraft, they could land almost anywhere.

Despite often not having any meteorological or topographical data to rely on, they did not get lost or have an accident. They also had good luck on their side as they never encountered an enemy aircraft. Nonetheless, they were in equal danger from Allied fighters or anti-aircraft gunners, who at a distance could have easily mistaken a Waco for an Italian CR.42 biplane.

The Air Section proved a success due to the solicitous handling, planning and maintenance procedures employed by two very skilled pilots. They had become familiar with landings at Siwa, Kufra, Kharga, Heliopolis (Cairo), Jalo and numerous landing grounds both named or numbered or not identified on a map. It was interesting that neither Barker nor Prendergast ever received RNZAF or RAF pilot's wings for their service. In 1944, Lieutenant Colonel David Lloyd Owen put in a request to higher command for Captain Barker to receive Air Force wings to reflect his flying skills in high-risk zones, both geographical and war-related. However, this was turned down because he had never completed an official RNZAF flying training course! This despite the fact that by April 1944, Barker had flown 955 hours in many operational areas in Egypt, Libya, Sudan, Sicily and Italy, plus normal communication flying in Palestine, Syria and Cyprus. In retrospect, the LRDG should have designed their own pilots' and navigators' flying insignia!

The Big Waco AX695 ended its service on 24 April 1942. It swung on landing at Heliopolis, Cairo while being flown by RAF personnel on a flight test after undertaking maintenance work. It was damaged beyond repair. The Little Waco remained in service until the end of the war.

The LRDG Air Section employed two American Waco cabin aircraft for liaison, reconnaissance, delivering essential supplies and mail, plus short-range casualty evacuation. This aircraft, AX697, is preparing for take-off.

Waco Model YKC, AX697 being inspected with the aid of a Ford F30 truck. Trooper I.G. McCulloch is in the foreground. It was known as Little Waco, as its sister aircraft had a more powerful engine and larger cabin space. The 'bump' cowling was later replaced by a standard rounded cowling to improve engine cooling.

(**Opposite, above**) Waco AX697 being refuelled. Note the Kiwi symbol in the shield and the LRDG marking under the wing.

(**Above**) Y Patrol members assist with the inspection of the Waco AX695, Big Waco. Meanwhile, two crew on the ground plot a course. On long trips, the pilots had to fly with an aerial-trained LRDG truck navigator seated alongside.

(**Opposite, below**) The Egyptian aircraft company Misr Airways undertook most major servicing requirements on the Wacos, as occasionally did the RAF, whereas regular maintenance was done by the LRDG. They were piloted by Major G.L. Prendergast (third right) and Captain R.F.T. Barker (second right). They pose with the Misr air mechanics.

Patrol members have a meeting and rest beside Waco AX697 following a visit. They were sturdy reliable aircraft that could land almost anywhere.

Cockpit view of the Waco. They had no radio or direction-finding equipment and were not armed.

Taiserbo, 28 November 1942. Trooper P.J. Burke lays on the stretcher, injured with multiple ankle fractures after his truck had run over a land mine. He awaits evacuation by the Waco. Under the wing is the Medical Officer R.P. Lawson. Left: Trooper H.D. Mackay and Trooper A. Vincent. Note the LRDG markings on the fuselage.

Waco Model ZGC, AX695. It was a five-seater, powered by a 285hp seven-cylinder Jacobs L5 engine, known as the Big Waco because it was higher-rated than its sister aircraft AX697 with a 225hp Jacobs L4 engine. On 24 April 1942, it swung on landing at Heliopolis, Cairo and was damaged beyond repair. It was being flown by RAF personnel who had been undertaking maintenance work and flight tests.

Chapter Six

The Barce Raid

By the time of the Barce raid (Operation CARAVAN) in September 1942, the patrols were highly tuned in desert warfare and ready for combat, equal to their more aggressive Special Forces counterparts. While raids on airfields were usually the prerogative of the SAS who were specifically trained for such operations, the attack on the Italian-held airfield and town of Barce in northern Libya was solely an LRDG affair. It was part of a greater Special Forces' assault plan to distract attention from the El Alamein build-up. The orders stated: 'To cause the maximum amount of damage and disturbance to the enemy. Synchronized to take place with similar raids being carried out at Tobruk, Operation AGREEMENT, and Benghazi, Operation BIGAMY.'

The Operation CARAVAN commander was Major J.R. Easonsmith. He led the New Zealand T1 Patrol under Captain N.P. Wilder and the British Guards, G1 Patrol, under Captain J.A.L. Timpson. There was also an attachment, Major V. Peniakoff, Libyan Arab Force as intelligence officer, along with two Libyan Arab Force soldiers to act as spies in Barce. Vladimir Peniakoff later formed Popski's Private Army (PPA).

The force consisted of forty-seven men travelling in five jeeps and seventeen heavily-armed Chevrolet trucks. They had initial support from the Rhodesian S Patrol and the Heavy Section, supplying forward fuel and supply dumps to extend the long journey. It took eleven days travelling behind enemy lines, including the difficult crossing of two great sand seas to reach their target: a total of 1,858 kilometres over all types of desert terrain.

On the journey there was an accident when the G Patrol commander Captain Timpson and his driver Guardsman T. Wann drove over the top of a razorback sand dune at high speed. The jeep capsized, Wann broke his back and was paralyzed from the waist down. Timpson suffered head injuries. Fortunately, though, they were still in a position to be evacuated by air and Sergeant J. Dennis MM took over command of G1 Patrol.

Barce was a classic Italian colonial town near the coast. The landscape could be described as less of a desert, being mainly trees and rocky terrain, though it also had a large agricultural area that maintained both an Italian and Libyan population in productive work. By 12 September the column had reached the foothills of the Jebel

Akhdar mountain range. Easonsmith left a concealed truck filled with rations, water and fuel as an emergency rallying-point at Bir el Gerrari, 96 kilometres from the target. The following evening, as the patrols approached the outskirts of the town, they cut down all the telegraph wires and shot up the Italian police checkpoint at Sidi Bu Raui, though a sudden halt in the dark caused the T1 Patrol Breda gun truck to run into the back of the T1 radio truck. It put the Breda truck out of action with a damaged radiator, so it had to be stripped and left on the side of the road.

Barce was the base of the Italian army Barce Sector Command. This included an airfield housing the 35th Bombing Wing, equipped with mostly Cant Z 1007 tri-motor bombers, plus a reconnaissance squadron of mainly Caproni Ca.311 twin-engine observation/bomber aircraft. The ground forces consisted of a company of Italian Africa Police with Autoblinda AB 41 armoured cars, a company of Royal Carabineers, a Blackshirts section, a machine-gun battalion, an artillery battery of 6-pounder guns and a company of L3/35 two-man light tanks. In addition, there were several Savari cavalry squadrons that were Libyans under Italian command. Positioned far within their own lines, they would have considered themselves fairly safe from any ground force attack.

The patrols prepared for the raid by hiding out under the trees until midnight and then they set off. As they approached Barce, G Patrol turned into the town while T1 headed for the airfield. The Guards, led by Major Easonsmith and Sergeant Dennis, had taken the Italians completely by surprise as most were asleep. They shot up the army barracks, using the devastating fire-power from the 20mm Breda gun and the heavy .50 Vickers machine guns, plus the twin .303 aircraft Brownings and Vickers K machine-guns, causing shock, horror and destruction. Also as the opportunity arose, they threw grenades by hand or launched them with .303 rifle grenade dischargers. Transport, fuel and ammo dumps were destroyed and general havoc was created around the town, including an attack on the Italian HQ.

Meanwhile, T1 Patrol in their five heavily-armed Chevrolet trucks crashed through the airfield gate, shooting the Italian guards and any others who got in their way. They drove around the airfield targeting the thirty aircraft arranged in a semi-circle. Using a destructive cocktail of tracer, incendiary and explosive ammunition, they fired at each bomber in turn. From the tail-end truck, *Te Paki III*, Corporal M.H. Craw and Trooper K. Yealands jumped from their vehicle and placed Lewis time bombs on the aircraft that were not already on fire; dangerous work with explosions from burning planes and enemy fire, but they managed to destroy ten aircraft in that manner. They had two bombs left. One had a faulty fuse, so they joined them together and placed them on an Italian Fieseler Storch light plane, totally destroying it.

The enemy was now truly alerted and began to fire back, but in the confusion was generally aiming too high. It would have been difficult for the defenders to identify their attackers, who were always moving. The scene was chaotic. There were explosions and flames lighting up the darkness and the Italians feared shooting their own planes. The patrol then targeted the fuel dump, creating a great blaze and, assisted by that light, shot up the administration, hangar and Air Force barrack buildings.

They were on the airfield for nearly an hour before T1 withdrew into the darkness. Unbelievably, there were no casualties or any vehicles put out of action. Fortunately for the patrol, eight Italian L3/35 two-man tankettes were positioned at the opposite end of the airfield from where they had approached. The Italians thought any attack would come from the south, not from the main road into the town. The tanks tried to engage the LRDG, but the trucks were too fast. Also, the small tanks had limited vision and were cumbersome to operate under those night conditions.

The outcome of the raid was twenty-three aircraft destroyed or damaged. The Italian reports listed the following as lost or damaged: nine Cant Z 1007 bombers; eleven Caproni bombers (nine Caproni Ca.311, one Caproni Ca.112 and one Caproni Ca.309); one IMAM Ro.63 light aircraft; one Savoia-Marchetti SM79 and one Fi 156 Fieseler Storch. The Barce airfield and town buildings, transport, fuel and ammunition supplies were also destroyed or damaged.

Following the attacks, both patrols had arranged to meet at a rendezvous some distance from Barce at Sidi Selim. T1 Patrol was expecting the road by which they reached the airfield to be blocked, so they drove at high speed through the main street of the town. However, at the end of the road, two L3/35 light tanks were blocking the way. The lead truck *Tutira III*, driven by Captain Wilder, had its headlights full on, blinding the tank crew. This fortunately caused the Italians to fire their twin 8mm machine guns too high, but there was no room to turn around, so Wilder just put his foot down and drove his heavy Chevrolet truck into the side of one of the light tanks. It spun around and crashed into the other. His truck was crippled, but the collision created a space for the rest of the vehicles to get through. Patrol members then threw grenades into the tanks and knocked them out before moving on.

Wilder and his crew then jumped into a jeep but as it was circling a roundabout, the driver was blinded by the flash of the crew firing the twin Vickers K machine guns. The jeep hit the kerb and overturned, throwing the men out but trapping Wilder underneath. Fortunately another truck came along and the men successfully extracted him from under the vehicle. However, Wilder was injured, along with several other men.

Meanwhile elsewhere in the town, Corporal M.H. Craw in his truck *Te Paki III* encountered an Italian Autoblinda 41 armoured car firing its 20mm gun. The rounds hit the fuel cans in the back of the truck, setting it on fire. In an attempt to escape, the driver did a sharp turn around a tight corner and ended up crashing into the entrance of an air-raid shelter. The crew were all captured. Of the five T1 patrol vehicles that took part in the airfield attack, only two made it to the rendezvous at Sidi Selim. Six

New Zealanders had been captured in the town, leaving only ten who escaped, four of whom were wounded.

Both patrols joined up as a column now reduced to ten trucks and three jeeps. As they were escaping through a valley at high speed, they were ambushed by Savari cavalry. Using their 6.5mm Carcano bolt-action carbines, they fired from the hills overlooking the road. The LRDG employed all their weapons in return fire and ran the gauntlet at speed. One truck received a puncture. It stopped and in record time changed the tyre while still under attack. Despite the many hits on the trucks, the patrols were lucky to have escaped with all the vehicles still mobile and only three men wounded. It was the LRDG's multi machine-gun fire-power, raking the hillsides, that was enough to suppress the aim of the Libyan cavalry, who were forced to keep their heads down.

The next day the exhausted patrols hid out under trees and camouflaged their vehicles, with the men having a meal, resting, doing repairs, cleaning guns and looking after the wounded. However, spotter planes had been sent out at dawn looking for the raiders, which liaised with Savari mounted patrols searching the ground. Eventually six CR.42 Falco biplane fighters came over and targeted the general area where the LRDG were thought to be hiding. From mid-morning to dusk they strafed all areas of potential cover, returning to base to rearm and refuel and come back again. One CR.42 crashed for an unknown reason, but it was not the patrols as they were trying to remain concealed and not returning fire. By the end of the day some men had been hit by the strafing, including Wilder, making a total of eleven wounded. Incredibly though, none were killed. However, by the evening most of the vehicles were shot up and burning. All that remained was just one truck *Te Anau II* and two jeeps to carry thirty-three exhausted men, including the wounded, back to Kufra, a journey of 1,226 kilometres. They also had to contend with a meagre supply of food and water.

Easonsmith split the remaining men into smaller parties, both driving and walking, to avoid being seen by aircraft. They were heading for a truck kept aside 96 kilometres away at Bir el Gerrari. It was prudently placed as a supply reserve, hidden on the way to Barce in case of an escape need such as this.

Captain R.P. Lawson, the medical officer, travelled with the wounded and several others on *Te Anau II* and a jeep. Private D.P Warbrick, a highly-skilled driver, successfully drove the overladen vehicle right through the night at a good speed over tough terrain. The jeep, due to punctures and mechanical problems, was soon abandoned, which meant that now they were all on the one vehicle. They located the reserve truck and took supplies and fuel, finally arriving at an abandoned RAF landing ground, LG 125, where they rested. They were later found by Y Patrol and the wounded were air-lifted out. The truck *Te Anau II* eventually returned to Kufra. It had thirty-nine bullet or shrapnel holes in it.

The walking party led by Easonsmith had only one jeep and the men took turns riding in it. They reached the hidden supply truck after walking 130 kilometres, where they recovered the vehicle and finally met up with the Rhodesian S Patrol. Several men became separated from the main groups. Trooper F.W. Jopling, the T1 Patrol navigator, was tasked with leading nine Guardsmen out on foot. An odd decision, as Jopling was suffering a minor wound in his leg and should have gone with the wounded on the truck.

It was a tough and arduous trek. After four days Jopling and the exhausted Lance Corporal E. Gutteridge were slowing down the main party, which led to the others having to go on without them. The remaining two were very short of water and couldn't eat as their mouths were too dry and their tongues very sore. Jopling recorded: 'The saliva dries in my mouth and I have to scratch my lips, tongue and roof of my mouth with my fingernails to scrape it off.' Things got so bad that they were forced to drink their own urine, little as there was, to gain some moisture in the mouth. Late on the fifth day of their trek, they came across an Arab elder at his camp site and the men were given water and were able to rest up.

Unfortunately, by the sixth day the early signs of gangrene were evident in Jopling's leg as he had a lump in his groin. He still had a field dressing in his kit, so he boiled up some water and bandaged his leg. Luckily they met some more Libyan Arabs who took care of the two men. Jopling was respected by the Arabs because he had taken the trouble to learn their language and so they looked after him as best as they could.

By the seventh day, Jopling's leg became very swollen and was producing a foul smell. It was also very difficult for him to walk. A donkey was found to carry him and he was taken to an Arab doctor who cleaned and bathed the wound. It had become gangrenous and the doctor said he would get additional help the next day.

On the eighth day, the doctor told Jopling he was in need of urgent medical care, otherwise the infection would kill him. So the Arab arranged for Jopling and his companion to be surrendered to the Italians for their own good. Later, while in a field hospital, the Italian and German medical officers said the leg needed to be amputated. Jopling didn't understand either language, but fortunately for him the Arab doctor, who also spoke Italian, interpreted for Jopling. He then pleaded with the doctors through the Arab to give it one more day after treatment. They agreed to do so and, fortunately, his leg improved and amputation was no longer necessary. Jopling's knowledge of Arabic probably saved his life, or at least his leg, but he remained a prisoner for the rest of the war.

Overall, the cost to the LRDG was ten captured and eleven wounded or injured, some of whom were prisoners of war. There were also two Libyan Arab Force scouts who went missing in Barce. The mission set out with seventeen vehicles; however, it returned with only three: a jeep and the battle-damaged *Te Anau II*, plus the reserve truck picked up on the way back. Amazingly, there were no LRDG killed in action or by accident. Furthermore, Guardsmen R. Duncalfe and P. McNabola were forced to hide out for two months, sheltered by Arabs, before they were able to get back to their own lines.

The Italians, on the other hand, suffered a huge setback in their operations, with the loss of valuable aircraft and war matériel. In spite of this, their causalities were surprisingly light in the face of the incredible fire-power concentrated on them. Four were killed, fifteen wounded and one Libyan Savari was taken prisoner. He remained with T Patrol as a willing servant and interpreter for nearly a year. The operation was considered a success, because no LRDG members were killed and most eventually returned. The losses to the Group were more than balanced in relation to the damage caused by this small force. The attack came as a complete surprise to the Italians. Had their tanks and armoured cars been ready for action, the LRDG trucks could have been easily defeated because they were especially vulnerable when loaded with unprotected jerry cans of petrol plus explosives and ammunition.

Operation CARAVAN took the pressure off the Eighth Army in its preparation for the El Alamein offensive. The Axis forces now had to reinforce their rear bases and airfields against raiders, taking valuable units from the front line to do so. The two other operations launched at the same time – Operation AGREEMENT against Tobruk and Operation BIGAMY against Benghazi – were both costly failures with no gains made. The raid also produced the most gallantry awards for any one LRDG action: two DSOs, two MCs and four MMs.

Despite the considerable price paid by the LRDG, this small force had inflicted great material loss and psychological damage to a more formidable enemy, who had felt secure behind their lines. It encompassed all the elements of the difficulties of negotiating desert travel, skilful navigation, independent action, fortitude, evasion and survival against the odds; factors common to the success of many other LRDG operations.

Major J.R. ('Jake') Easonsmith stands alongside his Ford F30, late 1941. He was a highly-respected and brave British officer who commanded R1 Patrol. LRDG medical orderly Private Mick Allen wrote of his officer as 'The gamest and finest man in the desert!' In September 1942, under the command of Easonsmith, the LRDG T1 and G1 patrols launched Operation CARAVAN, an attack on the Italian-held airfield and town of Barce.

(**Opposite, above**) T1 Patrol trucks lined up displaying the Maori names on the vehicles. *Tutira III* on the left was Captain N.P. Wilder's truck. The Chevrolet was later put out of action after crashing into two light tanks while attempting to break through a Barce town roadblock.

(**Opposite, below**) Trooper A. Vincent cleans his jeep-mounted Vickers K machine gun. These were originally RAF air gunners' weapons adopted by the LRDG and used in single or dual mounts. With a 100-round enclosed magazine, they were very effective, producing devastating fire-power of 950 to 1,200 rounds per minute. Dust meant that the weapons had to be covered as much as possible and regularly cleaned. Note the flare pistol on the bonnet.

(**Above**) Trooper F.W. Jopling was the chief navigator responsible for guiding the column on their two-week journey to Barce. Here he employs a theodolite to help plot his position. After the battle, he was slightly wounded in the withdrawal from the town. However, following a ten-day trek terminating with a gangrenous leg, he was captured and recovered from his wounds.

(**Above**) A rear view of Captain J.A.L. Timpson's Willys jeep driven by Guardsman T. Wann (pictured). Note the twin Vickers K mounted in front. On the outward journey, the jeep capsized while crossing a large razorback dune. Captain Timpson suffered head injuries and Guardsman Wann broke his back. They were both evacuated by aircraft.

(**Opposite, above**) Captain Timpson having his head injuries dressed by the Medical Officer Captain R.P. Lawson. He sits in front of the Guards truck G2. Note the spare tyre roped to the grille.

(**Opposite, below**) Sergeant J. Dennis took over command of G1 Patrol. He drives his jeep with Guardsman R. Duncalfe behind the twin Vickers K guns. Note the EY grenade-launcher rifle behind Dennis. This weapon was used in the attack on Barce town and the Italian barracks. Grenades were launched through doors, windows and into trenches.

A heavily-loaded jeep with jerry cans of fuel and water on the way to Barce. Major Easonsmith takes notes in the shade of the vehicle. The covered twin Vickers K guns were used later with great effect when he shot up Barce town. He destroyed ten vehicles, plus a fuel tanker and trailer.

Major Vladimir Peniakoff rests on his jeep on the way to Barce. He acted as Intelligence Officer with two Libyan Arab Force members who served as spies. While fleeing Barce with the patrols, Peniakoff lost a finger through enemy fire while escaping an ambush. He later formed Popski's Private Army.

While on their eleven-day journey to Barce, T1 Patrol trucks line up at the edge of the Great Sand Sea. Over the two patrols, the mission set out with five jeeps and twelve trucks. However, of those that saw action, only one truck T6, *Te Anau II*, the fitter's truck (on the right) returned, along with a jeep. One truck was concealed outside Barce as a supply/rescue rendezvous point. The rest were lost to enemy action, accident or breakdown.

The LRDG column close to Barce. The vehicle on the right is the Breda gun truck. This was put out of action due to an accident in the dark, when one vehicle ran into the back of another.

Captain Wilder holds a map while he addresses his men in preparation for the attack on Barce airfield. The men are looking vigilant, looking out for an enemy aircraft that was flying overhead at the time. Later, T1 patrol attacked the airfield at night and destroyed or damaged twenty-three aircraft on the ground, plus fuel and munitions dumps.

Captain N.P. Wilder (standing centre) reads the operational orders to his men as they enjoy their evening meal. They are hidden under the trees in the outskirts of Barce in preparation for the attack that night. The bald soldier on the extreme left is Major V. Peniakoff.

Corporal M.H. Craw, T1 Patrol. He stands draped in machine-gun belts in front of an old 1938 Ford V8 used as a base runabout at Siwa. Later on the Barce Raid, he won the Military Medal for personally destroying ten aircraft with time-bombs. He was later captured, but escaped a year later.

An Italian L3/35 (Carro Veloce CV 35) two-man light tank armed with twin 8mm machine guns. T Patrol encountered these on the airfield raid, but in the darkness was easily outmanoeuvred. To clear a way through, Captain Wilder had to crash his truck into a pair of them serving as a roadblock in Barce town. The light tanks were then put out of action with hand grenades.

(**Opposite, above**) Corporal M.H. Craw's truck T5, *Te Paki III*, was hit by enemy fire in Barce town and crashed. Some of the crew were injured and all taken prisoner. The truck was burned out. See the destroyed stores in the back, a .50 Vickers heavy machine gun, plus a Vickers K on the ground.

(**Opposite, below**) The underside view of *Te Paki III*. The box fixed to the side held the time-bombs used by Corporal Craw in the airfield attack. The wreck is a curiosity for the locals, who the night before would have kept their heads down when the town was shot up by G1 Patrol.

(**Above**) Trooper R.E. Hay behind his .303 Vickers heavy machine gun. He was captured in Barce, as part of the crew of the crashed *Te Paki III*. He bravely rescued Trooper K. Yealands, who was badly wounded lying in the back of the burning truck.

Captain Wilder's truck *Tutira III* in Italian hands. While escaping the airfield raid, he crashed his truck into two Italian L3 light tanks as he broke through a roadblock. The crippled vehicle was abandoned and the crew transferred to jeeps.

(**Opposite, above left**) Captain R.P. ('Dick') Lawson MC. Known as 'Doc' among the troops, he was a long-serving LRDG medical officer. He served on the Barce raid and won the Military Cross for sheltering the wounded while under fire from air attack. Lawson later participated in the Aegean Dodecanese operations in 1943. After the fall of Leros, he was captured and went on to organize the medical arrangements for the wounded prisoners of war.

(**Opposite, below**) *Te Anau II* was the sole surviving truck after the raid. It carried the wounded on a long and dangerous journey to a landing ground, where the men were evacuated by air. It was overloaded with weapons and stores acquired from other vehicles, plus the wounded. Most of the patrol trucks were put out of action in the battle or the following day by air attack while escaping the town. Major Peniakoff stands next to the well, while the driver Private D.P. Warbrick is seated.

(**Opposite, above right**) Private J.L.D. Davis navigated *Te Anau II* in taking the wounded to Landing Ground 125 for rescue. The *keffiyeh* was only worn in North Africa, being replaced by a black beret as the official headdress from mid-1943. Davis went on to serve with distinction in the Aegean operations of late 1943 and was awarded the British Empire Medal.

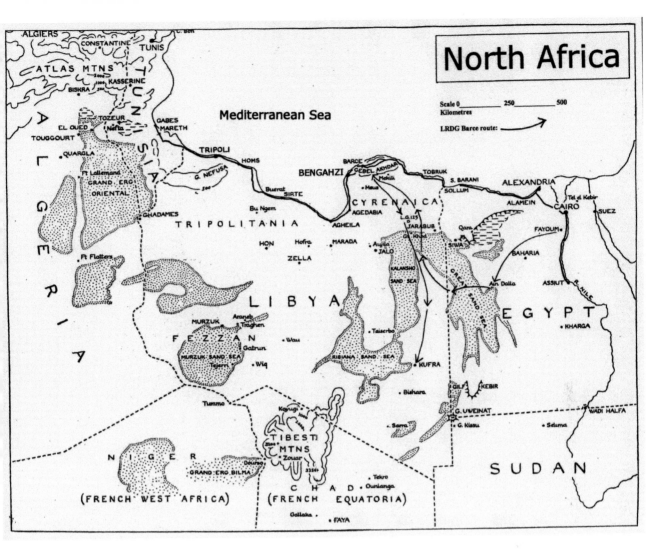

North Africa

Scale 0   250   500
Kilometres

LRDG Barce route:

(**Opposite, above**) Barce airfield re-visited in 1943. The destroyed aircraft can still be seen in the background.

(**Opposite, below**) Barce liberated by the Allies, 1943. During the 1942 raid, while T1 Patrol attacked the airfield, Major Easonsmith and G1 Patrol under Sergeant Dennis shot up the town including vehicles, supplies and the military barracks. Note the Italian building boldly marked 'Duce'.

(**Above**) Map of North Africa where the arrow lines indicate the route taken on the Barce raid in September 1942. The outward journey took eleven days and included the difficult crossing of two great sand seas.

Chapter Seven

The Final Days in the Desert

The Eighth Army entered Tripoli on 23 January 1943. The rapid advance of 2,250 kilometres in three months had made it necessary for the LRDG to move its base from Kufra, 965 kilometres north-westwards to Zella and later another 240 kilometres to Hon. These moves from one place to the next were successfully completed by the trucks of the Heavy Section in a single journey.

Part of the success of the LRDG were their often 'unsung heroes' the fitters, who over the three years of desert operations kept the vehicles serviced to the highest standard. Their skills were crucial to the survival of the patrols and the success of their missions. Each patrol carried a fitter, along with a dedicated truck that carried the tools and spares to undertake what field maintenance and repairs they could. The other fitters were based at the LRDG HQ workshops. As soon as a patrol returned to base, the trucks were handed over to the Light Repair Section. They would immediately undertake service and inspection work to ensure that the trucks were ready again for action at short notice. Each vehicle was overhauled every six months, and the engines usually did between 19,000 and 26,000 kilometres before they were replaced.

One New Zealander, Staff Sergeant A.F. McLeod, who first served as a fitter in the Heavy Section and then later in charge of A Squadron workshops at Abbassia, received the British Empire Medal for his diligence in overseeing the repair and maintenance of the Group's trucks and equipment. The workshops also worked closely with the gunners in creating and installing special truck mounts for weapons like wreck-recovered .303 aircraft Browning machine guns and other armaments.

The fitters in the British patrols were specialists from the Royal Army Ordnance Corps. The New Zealanders usually supplied the fitters from their own units. Their skills were reflected in an allowance of an extra shilling a day. In July 1941, as part of an official dispatch concerning an appreciation of LRDG activities, General Wavell gave special praise to the fitters, both in the workshops and in the field:

Their exploits have been achieved only by careful organisation, and a very high standard of enterprise, discipline, mechanical maintenance and desert navigation. A special word of praise must be added for the RAOC fitters whose work contributed so much to the mechanical endurance of the vehicles in such unprecedented conditions.

One of the last significant desert actions of the Group was supporting the Eighth Army advance into Tunisia. In preparation for this, it was required to reconnoitre and map the country's southern approaches through which a column would have to pass, outflanking the Axis-held Mareth Line. In January and February 1943, the LRDG and Indian Long Range Squadron explored the territory to the south and west of the range of hills extending southwards from Matmata. As they progressed the patrols signalled HQ daily, reporting the 'going', obstacles, cover, water supply and sites for landing grounds. On their return, the commanders conferred with LRDG Intelligence Officer Captain L.H. Browne at the NZ Division HQ, where a model was made to demonstrate possible lines of advance.

On 12 January, T1 Patrol under Captain N.P. Wilder crossed the frontier and became the first troops of the Eighth Army to enter Tunisia. They found an uncharted pass south through the Matmata Hills, which became known as Wilder's Gap. It was by this route, two months later, that the NZ Division executed its 'left hook' round the fortified Mareth Line. Other patrols explored the country further to the west: T2 in the area to the south of Djebel Tebaga between Matmata and Chott el Djerid, a high salt marsh; while G2 was in the area between the Chott and the Grand Erg Oriental, an impassable sand sea extending into southern Algeria.

The final task assigned to the LRDG by the Eighth Army was the navigation of the New Zealand Corps during the outflanking of the Mareth Line in March 1943. Appropriately the work was performed by New Zealanders, Captain R.A. Tinker with three men from T2 Patrol in two jeeps, who would be acting as guides. The New Zealand Corps passed through Wilder's Gap and remained at an assembly area, while the route was plotted to the north-west. A wadi with steep, rocky escarpments presented a very difficult obstacle but Tinker, accompanied by New Zealand engineers, found a place where tracks could be constructed with road-making machinery to get heavy transport across.

Meanwhile the T2 navigator, Corporal D.M. Bassett DCM, guided a New Zealand Provost party marking the 'Diamond Track' using cut-out drums enclosing candles or lanterns which would light the line of advance at night. As the corps left the assembly area on 19 March, in recognition of Bassett's navigational skills which made this operation possible, Lieutenant General Bernard Freyberg, NZ Corps commander, invited Corporal Bassett to sit alongside him in his jeep to watch progress. The following day, the Eighth Army launched its frontal attack on the Mareth Line. From there they moved forward to Tebaga, along the route reconnoitred by the Group, and made contact with the enemy on 21 March. Eventually the Axis forces were driven back to a corner of Tunisia, ending with their final surrender in North Africa on 13 May 1943.

There being no further scope for the LRDG, they were released from the Eighth Army and returned to Egypt to rest and reorganize.

In a letter dated 2 April 1943, General Bernard Montgomery wrote to the LRDG commander, Colonel G.L. Prendergast, of his appreciation of the work of the Group:

> I would like you to know how much I appreciate the excellent work done by your patrols and by the SAS in reconnoitring the country up to the Gabès Gap. Without your careful and reliable reports the launching of the 'left hook' by the NZ Division would have been a leap in the dark; with the information they provided, the operations could be planned with some certainty, and as you know, went off without a hitch.

An additional tribute came from Winston Churchill in Volume IV of his *The Second World War* histories written after the war, in which he gave full credit to the LRDG for their role in this operation as follows:

> The route had formerly been pronounced by the French as impossible for vehicles, but had been reconnoitred in January by the Long Range Desert Group and declared feasible, if very difficult. Here was not the least valuable of the many services rendered throughout the African campaign by this hardy and mobile reconnaissance unit.

An overall appreciation of the LRDG came on 13 May 1943, the day the Axis forces surrendered in North Africa, when as part of a message sent by General Alexander to Winston Churchill, the following was stated:

> The victory had taken three years, many battles and much sacrifice; of the formations engaged, the desert raiders of the LRDG and SAS formed numerically a minute part. But it is true to say that without their efforts, victory would have come later at a far greater cost. Their role in the history of warfare remains unique.

(**Opposite, above**) S Patrol vehicle with a stencil-painted scorpion on the bonnet. Private A.F. Goddard stands alongside.

(**Opposite, below**) Afrika Korps prisoners and Libyan drivers captured by the LRDG. In the background are the British Bedford trucks the Germans were driving when taken.

LRDG R Patrol desert meeting, 11 December 1942. They pose with (centre, left to right) Generals Freyberg and Montgomery. On the right, Captain L.H. ('Tony') Browne MM, DCM, patrol commander. He stands with his patrol.

Y Patrol trucks left – *Chattanooga Choo Choo* and *Nemesis* – travel in the rain through Tocri Pass, Cyrenaica.

(**Above, left**) Sergeant R.W.N. ('Dick') Lewis photographed in Cairo in early 1943.

(**Above, right**) Sergeant Lewis: the transformation after a six-week mission in the desert. A strict water ration prevented regular shaving.

(**Left**) LRDG fitters undertake repair and maintenance work in an outdoor workshop in Kufra. These men kept the vehicles, weapons and equipment maintained to a high standard to ensure reliable desert travel and equipment.

R Patrol members at the A (NZ) Squadron HQ workshops in 1943. The truck on the left is an original patrol Ford 01 V8, HQ6. Note the Vickers gun chest in the rear of the vehicle. Sitting right, Trooper A.F. Dodunski; standing right, Private A.F. Brown; other men unidentified.

The LRDG Light Repair Section, Lebanon1943. The men pose in front of a vehicle recovery truck. Third from left, Private A. Tighe MM, MiD; fifth left, Private L. Sullivan, Y Patrol.

LRDG fitters in the Light Repair Section. These men carried out the vital work of maintaining LRDG transport to the highest standard. Back row, left: Private W.G. Bambury, Sapper J.P. Gilmore, Private C.I. McConachie, Private F.R. McCallum, Private F.R. Stone, Private D.A. Lewis and Private D. Farmer. Front row: Private N.W. Gedye, Private N.J. Parker, Private R.H. Crabbe and Private L.D. Dalziel.

A (NZ) Squadron fitters stand alongside a restored 1938 Ford 01 V8 at the Light Repair Section base, 1943. Left: Private F.R. Stone and Private L.D. Dalziel. Note the scorpion symbol on the vehicle.

Left: Sergeant W.H. Rail and Trooper S.D. Parker stand in front of a well-concealed truck. They are suitably dressed and equipped as they are about to set out on a foot reconnaissance after crossing into Tunisia in January 1943. Note Parker is carrying a 9mm Sten gun. A very unusual submachine gun to see in North Africa, especially in the LRDG where the mainstay weapon was the .45 Thompson.

T1 Patrol, 12 January 1943. They were the first troops of the Eighth Army to enter Tunisia. They crossed the frontier south of the Matmata Hills, finding a pass that became known as Wilder's Gap. They erected a marker made from jerry cans with the word 'Tunisia'. From left to right, back row: Lieutenant E.Y.M. Hutchinson, Trooper H.D. Mackay, Sergeant Major W. Morrison, Trooper K.E. Tippett, Trooper N.W. Hobson and Sergeant R.W.N. Lewis. Middle: Captain N.P. Wilder, Trooper A. Vincent, Corporal J.L.D. Davis, Sergeant W.H. Rail and Dr Holywood RAMC. Front: Private S.D. Parker, Trooper E.R. Dobson, Private R.D. Tant and Private D.B. Warbrick.

LRDG rugby football team, Azizia, near Tripoli, March 1943. It was captained by Charlie Saxton, patrol commander and ex-rugby All Black. The team, back row, left to right: Captain K.F. ('Paddy') McLauchlan, Major A.I. Guild, Trooper K.E. Tippett, Trooper A.F. Dodunski, Private F.J. Whitaker, Trooper R.A. Davison, Private D.O. Beale and Trooper J.H.E. Taylor. Front row, left to right: Private R.D. Tant, Trooper N.W. Hobson, Trooper H.H. Cleaver, Lieutenant C.K. Saxton, Lance Corporal C.A. Yaxley, Corporal J.L.D. Davis, Trooper A.Connelly and Corporal E.F. Gorringe. Lying in front: Trooper R. Larkin.

AGAINST IMPOSSIBLE ODDS

This is the story of a victory won against odds that made it seem impossible by men of the Long Range Desert Group. It is told by Eric Bigio, "Daily Express" War Correspondent

In May 1943, the *Parade* magazine published a story about the work of the LRDG. The headline sums it up! The men pictured are from the Yeomanry Y2 Patrol. Left to right: Troopers B. Bullock and F. ('Jankers') Johns and Corporal R. ('Nobby') Hall.

Chapter Eight

The Dodecanese Operations: The Aegean, 1943

By May 1943, after serving in the desert since its first operation in September 1940, the LRDG had finished its work following the surrender of the Axis forces in Tunisia. During this time there was much speculation among the troops as to where the LRDG would be going next. The Group's commander, Colonel G.L. Prendergast, had paid several visits (in the LRDG Waco liaison aircraft which he piloted) to GHQ Middle East to discuss the future of the unit. After much discussion, the meeting came out strongly against disbandment because of the difficulty in re-training specialist personnel should the necessity occur. It was agreed that the LRDG ought not to be disbanded, but should continue to operate in Europe on much the same lines as before. A revised establishment plan was to be drawn up.

Much reorganization was undertaken at Alexandria before the two squadrons eventually moved on to their new training ground in the Lebanon. With the three-year desert war finally over, many long-serving veterans returned home on furlough or rejoined their parent units. This meant further recruitment and re-establishment of the squadrons. Nevertheless, they were never short of volunteers. The reputation of the LRDG as an elite force had been well recognized, hence the desire to join by those looking for something different from the constraints of the regular army.

It was also found necessary to disband the long-serving Guards G Patrol owing to the difficulty in finding suitable personnel from the Guards Brigade, which had suffered severe casualties in Tunisia. The existing G Patrol members formed new patrols along with members of the Heavy Section, whose trucks were no longer required. They became M1 and M2 Patrols or joined HQ as drivers, all as part of B Squadron.

On 1 April 1943, the LRDG received a directive that required the unit to be able to operate by jeep or on foot in mountainous country with the object of liaison with patriot forces. Thus it became necessary for the Group to readjust its thinking and arrange a comprehensive training programme. The second-in-command, Major J.R. Easonsmith, travelled to Syria to find a suitable training ground. He was fortunate to be able to arrange to take over the Cedars Hotel, which was a peacetime ski resort in the Lebanon mountains previously used as the Middle East Ski School.

From May 1943, the LRDG A and B Squadrons spent nearly three and a half months training at the picturesque Cedars of Lebanon. The patrols were reorganized into small self-contained units, varying from four to eight men depending on their task. They had to be capable of maintaining communications over distances of 160 kilometres while operating covertly behind enemy lines on foot. This was a radical departure from nearly three years of relying on transport to now having to walk to complete their mission. The stamina and fitness levels required were of an exceptional standard, so some desert veterans who were unable to make the transition had to return to their original units.

After eight weeks' preparation, the men could do a climbing trek of 27 kilometres with 14kg packs, while after three months they were achieving 100–160 kilometres carrying pack and weapon weights of 30–36kg. Bergen rucksacks were employed to manage these loads. Other packs known as Everest carrier frames, designed to support heavy wireless sets or batteries, were also used. The patrols were issued with a new lighter type of radio, the US-made Collins 18M Transmitter-Receiver Field Set. They replaced the reliable No. 11 sets that had served them well in the desert.

As part of the reorganization, their beloved Chevrolet trucks were gone, apart from some reserved for general transport duties by HQ. However, a proportion of jeeps mounting .50 calibre Browning machine guns were still retained. These were used only where the terrain and the operation were appropriate. The Group now essentially functioned as small foot patrols, similar to a Commando/SAS-type operation. They continued with their primary skill set of intelligence-gathering and reconnaissance work. At the Cedars, the patrols usually consisted of one officer, one sergeant, three qualified signallers and two general duty men, including one combat soldier also qualified as a medical orderly.

The men were taught mountain-climbing and warfare, demolitions, cross-country skiing, parachuting and the handling of pack mules. Some were also educated in basic German and Greek so they could seek the assistance of the local people when needed. Each patrol had to have at least one man who could speak Greek. Since they were independent units, they had to carry all their own supplies. As well as this, they were trained to be capable of living behind enemy lines, under probably difficult and extreme conditions, for up to a month. They also had to be proficient in maintaining continued wireless communications with base HQ.

On 10 September, while A Squadron was absent from the Cedars on a vessel seaborne-landing exercise in Cyprus, an urgent message was received from Middle East Command. It stated that the whole unit was required immediately for operations in the Italian-occupied Dodecanese Islands in the Aegean. The uncompleted B Squadron parachute course at Ramat David was also abandoned and the personnel had to be ready to sail within twenty-four hours. Consequently, on 11 September the LRDG, comprising 212 officers and other ranks, moved from the Cedars to the port of Haifa in Palestine. No LRDG transport was taken, so requisitions were made to obtain a quantity of .303 Bren guns as all the existing heavier .50 calibre machine guns were designed to fit onto the unit's jeeps. The Bren gun was to be the mainstay light machine gun used by the patrols in the Aegean operations. After more than three months' training in the mountains and developing specialist skills, the men were at a very high level of fitness and eager for their next deployment. By the time the order came to move, the men were both physically and mentally ready to apply their newly-honed Special Forces' skills.

Following the Italian armistice in September 1943, British forces began to occupy the Dodecanese Islands in the Aegean Sea between Greece and Turkey. The armistice was a consequence of the overthrow of *Il Duce* ('the Leader') Benito Mussolini in July 1943 and his being replaced by Marshal Pietro Badoglio. Britain's Prime Minister Winston Churchill saw it as an opportunity to open a new front in the eastern Mediterranean. He thought such a strategy could only add more pressure on Hitler's stretched military forces, already fighting on many fronts. It might also provide encouragement for Turkey to join the Allies. However, General Dwight Eisenhower refused to give American support, considering it a waste of time and resources and not a priority for Allied forces at that time. He stated that they were already heavily committed with the invasions in Sicily and Italy and had no ships to spare.

Nonetheless undeterred, Churchill went ahead on 9 September and approved the plan code-named Operation ACCOLADE. He cabled Middle East Command with the words: 'This is a time to play high. Improvise and dare.' Churchill concluded that the island of Rhodes with its vital airfields offered the key to the command of the Aegean and ultimately Turkey's decision to enter the war. However, the Germans also had plans to occupy the islands, so the race began.

The day after Italy capitulated on 6 September, the Germans began to occupy all the main Italian-held islands. By 13 September, German troops controlled Rhodes and its vital air bases. This immediately put Churchill's plan in jeopardy because it left only Kos, with its small airfield, as the sole RAF fighter cover for operations in the Dodecanese. However, in early October that was also taken by the Germans. The Luftwaffe had massed approximately 400 planes mostly based in Greece, whereas the nearest significant British airfield was on Cyprus, 435 kilometres distant. North African airfields were beyond the range of single-engine fighters. In the main, only RAF Bristol Beaufighters and DC-3 Dakota transports were able to assist in their respective attack and supply roles. The Luftwaffe dominance meant that throughout the islands, most British destroyers and smaller vessels were only able to re-supply and transport troops under the cover of night.

The LRDG became part of the Raiding Forces, Middle East, which was made up of around 200 LRDG, 150 men of the SBS and No. 30 Commando. Colonel G.L. Prendergast was appointed second-in-command of the Raiding Forces and

Lieutenant Colonel J.R. Easonsmith was promoted to Officer Commanding LRDG. The New Zealand (A) Squadron was commanded by Major A.J. Guild and B Squadron, the British and Rhodesians, were led by Major D.L. Lloyd Owen. They were to be used to support some 3,000 regular British troops of 234 Brigade holding the islands, under the command of Major General F.G.R. 'Ben' Brittorous as Leros Fortress commander, later replaced by Brigadier R.A.G Tilney.

The island outposts were manned by detachments of the SBS and the LRDG. The Group had set up watches on the islands of Astypalaia (Stampalia), Kos, Kythnos, Mykonos, Naxos, Gyaros, Serifos and Symi. They acted as observers in the outlying islands astride the sea and air routes to the Dodecanese to report the movements of enemy shipping and aircraft. Many of these islands were occupied by the Germans at some point, so the patrols had to keep well-concealed and often had to withdraw with some narrow escapes when discovered. This important coast-watch role of reporting all observations was a job similar to the famous Road Watch employed in the North African campaign. Between September and November 1943, the gathering and transmitting of this vital intelligence of sea and air activity was one of the primary tasks of the LRDG Aegean operations.

For transport around the islands, modified Greek sailing/fishing vessels called caiques were used, which ranged in size from small to large twin-masted schooners. They were manned by the Royal Navy along with army personnel employed as gunners. Known as the Levant Schooner Flotilla (LSF), they were under the command of Lieutenant Commander Adrian Seligman, with an operational fleet of twelve vessels that were identified as LS1 to LS12. Their task was to carry detachments of the LRDG, SBS and Commandos to missions throughout the islands and later to pick them up again. Due to the covert nature of the work, often undertaken within enemy-occupied areas, most sailing had to be navigated at night. During the day, they would lay close inshore in coves, where the boats were camouflaged with netting to blend in with the rocky coastline. Royal Navy Motor Launches (MLs) were also employed as required.

The LRDG suffered their greatest loss in one action with the assault on the island of Levitha on 23 October. This ill-conceived operation lasted nearly two days and cost the Group five killed and thirty-seven taken prisoner, with only seven escaping the island. Of the former, nineteen captured and four killed or missing were New Zealanders. The patrols were ordered by the brigade commander to embark on an infantry assault mission to take the small island occupied by the enemy. It was thought to be defended in low numbers. Yet despite protest from the LRDG commanders, initial reconnaissance was not permitted to confirm this. Furthermore, the men did not normally operate as infantrymen as they were specifically trained as specialists, skilled in intelligence-gathering and covert operations. Nonetheless, they undertook the mission and landed under the cover of darkness. At first a steady advance was made, taking enemy positions, and a good fight was mounted, capturing many prisoners. Eventually, they were worn down and had to surrender to an overwhelming force, which attacked from both the ground and air. It was a big setback for the LRDG as almost a third of its members had become casualties or were taken prisoner; a tragic waste of specialist troops, more so when several thousand British servicemen were still based on Leros. A brigade infantry assault would have been more fitting for the task.

The losses caused an immediate flurry within the New Zealand government because it was revealed that their troops had been consigned to the Aegean without official approval. The government required that it had to be consulted first before its soldiers were committed to a new theatre of war. Further discussions with the British government concluded that the New Zealanders would be permanently withdrawn from the LRDG. It was agreed, therefore, that the A (NZ) Squadron LRDG would be pulled out as soon as the tactical situation allowed, though they remained in Leros until its capitulation on 16 November.

The regular air-raids and final assault on Leros lasted for almost fifty days and nights from 23 September to 16 November. The actual invasion on 12 November led to five exhausting days of fighting, as both sides lost and re-took ground in a series of see-saw actions. It was a very violent clash with much close-quarter fighting, along with extensive bombing resulting in significant casualties. In this conflict, the LRDG was also one of the few military units where majors and colonels led patrols into combat and fought alongside their men. They equally shared all the privations and hardships, and some were killed in action including their commander Lieutenant Colonel J.R. Easonsmith and S Patrol commander Major A.G. Redfern.

Five LRDG patrols were assigned to the Italian gun battery positions, employing the heights as coastal observation points but also to stiffen the morale of their new allies, ensuring the guns and their crews performed effectively. Initially the coastal defences gave good service, but were eventually knocked out by regular Luftwaffe dive-bombing attacks. The patrols that were not employed at observation points and/ or overseeing the coastal gun batteries were formed into independent reconnaissance and fighting units, patrolling by day and night. Essentially they were in an anti-paratroops role, moving between combat zones more quickly than the regular troops were able, supplying information and providing support as required.

The British troops were especially worn down. Their ammunition was running low, and many suffered from thirst; even though there was sufficient water on the island, access was difficult. Battle conditions often caused the failure of essential supplies and ammunition from reaching the front lines, or caused them to become erratic in receipt. After five days of sustained fighting, on the evening of 16 November, the Brigade HQ at Meraviglia was taken and the Fortress Commander Brigadier Tilney was forced to surrender. The Germans had total unopposed dominance of the air, which was the main factor in their victory over Leros. According to German records, on Kos and Leros combined, almost 4,600 British service personnel were taken prisoner, along with another 357 troops killed. The Italians suffered the worst, with approximately 8,500 captured and an unknown number killed.

Of the LRDG, over their three months on the islands, twelve were killed in action, including its commander and two were missing, presumed dead. Another later died in England as a result of serious injuries from a jeep accident on Leros. In addition, about 120 patrolmen were captured and one later died while a prisoner. In all, almost two-thirds of the LRDG committed to the Dodecanese operations were lost, though many did manage to escape the enemy by employing their specialist evasion skills. They had refused to surrender, and continued fighting or evading the enemy until they could get away.

The Dodecanese operations proved to be the last action that A (NZ) Squadron was to undertake with the LRDG. After that debacle, the Group transferred to a new base at Azzib, north of Haifa in Palestine, to rest and reorganize. On orders from the New Zealand government, due to the losses, the squadron was to disband on 31 December 1943. However, prior to this, the Christmas celebrations were some-what prolonged as there was a party almost every night as memories were shared and farewells exchanged with their British and Rhodesian comrades.

The final break-up dinner was on Friday night, 14 January 1944, and the next day in Cairo the squadron was officially wound up. Most of its members, if they did not go home on furlough, spent time at the New Zealand Armoured Corps Training Depot in Egypt. From there they were posted as reinforcements to the Divisional Cavalry with the 2nd New Zealand Division in Italy.

By December 1943 the Group, under the command of Lieutenant Colonel D.L. Lloyd Owen DSO, MC was reorganized into two squadrons, each of eight patrols consisting of one officer and ten men. To replace the New Zealanders, a new A (Rhodesian) Squadron was formed under the command of Captain K.H. Lazarus MBE. He had earned much credit as a surveyor in mapping the Libyan sands and later as a patrol commander. The British B Squadron was commanded by Captain M.P. Stormonth-Darling.

To ensure the LRDG did not lose its high level of expertise, Lieutenant General Freyberg allowed Lloyd Owen to retain several long-serving New Zealand members. Initially they were Captain L.H. Browne MC, DCM (he was made the Group's Intel-ligence Officer); Captain R.A. Tinker MC, MM was second-in-command of B Squad-ron; Captain C.H. Croucher was appointed Officer Commanding, Boats; Captain D.J. Aitken, Patrol Commander, X1 Patrol; and Captain R.J. Landon-Lane, Patrol Com-mander, X2 Patrol. Also Private L.J. Hawkins was retained as a fitter employed in the workshops. Later, Captain K.F. McLauchlan and Sergeant M.H. Craw also rejoined. Most of these men had already served the Group with much distinction.

Two new bases were established at Bari and Rodi in southern Italy. Bari was the main operational HQ till the end of the war, and it was from there that most of the missions were planned and directed. Rodi, though a long way from Bari, was a good site for base communications and a quiet place for the men to rest after operations. By May 1944, after months of diverse and specialized training, which included the handling of pack mules and small boats, parachuting, mountain warfare, skiing and how to operate in snow conditions (snowshoe skills), they were ready for the first of many intrusions into enemy-occupied territory. Their initial actions were behind the lines in Italy, and from then on until the end of the war patrols operated in Yugoslavia, Albania, Greece, the Dalmatian Islands, Istria and Croatia.

The Group maintained its intelligence-gathering and reconnaissance role, but also operated with local partisans in many sabotage and hit-and-run actions. The LRDG set up coast watches to report on enemy shipping as targets for Allied naval and air commands. In addition they planned, often in conjunction with the SBS, small-scale raids against enemy shipping in harbours and island garrisons. Objectives were reached either by parachute or by sea. By the middle of September 1944, there were a total of eighteen different parties on various tasks stretching from the north-east corner of Italy through Yugoslavia and Albania to Greece. The organization and control of these operations was complex and their success did not only lie with the men in the field but also in the care and skill of the planners at LRDG HQ.

For operations around the Dalmatian islands the LRDG could not always rely on the Royal Navy for assistance at short notice, so they created their own shipping fleet of two motor fishing vessels, the MFV *La Palma* and MFV *Kufra*. Both were armed and had a good carrying capacity for communication systems, men, stores and equipment. These robust vessels with their LRDG crews performed much valuable work. A Waco liaison aircraft was still in service and flown by New Zealander Captain R.F.T. Barker. Along with the Group's vessels, it was probably one of the few Special Forces units in the Second World War that could boast its own Air Force and navy!

By the time the war had ended in Europe, the Group had completed more than 100 successful operations. Allied Forces HQ recommended that the LRDG should continue its role in the Far East. The response for volunteers had been impressive. At one time more than 300 members of the unit were prepared to go, with half that number volunteering to defer their release from the army to do so. Consequently, on 16 June 1945 they were ordered as a unit back to England, where they were to regroup and go on leave before being sent to Asia. There was even talk of operating in the Gobi desert. However, a week later Lloyd Owen received a War Office signal stating that the LRDG was to be disbanded. It was received as sad and disappointing news by the Group.

On 1 August, five years and fourteen days after its formation in Cairo, what began as Ralph Bagnold's small reconnaissance force ceased to exist. During those years the

LRDG achieved a great measure of success, making a significant contribution in their diverse areas of operations. This was out of all proportion to the size of the unit and the number of casualties they suffered. A few who had joined the unit as 'other ranks' in June 1940 still remained in June 1945, all New Zealanders: Captain L.H. Browne MC, DCM; Captain R. Tinker MC, MM; Captain R.J. Landon-Lane; Captain C.H.B. Croucher MiD and Private L. Hawkins.

There were also others who had been with the Group for more than four years, whose contribution to the growth and proficiency of the force during that time had been outstanding. They had seen the unit operating in unarmoured vehicles behind the lines in Libya, training on skis in the mountains of Syria and Italy, being dropped by parachute over Italy and the Balkans, and landing by sea in the Aegean, Ionian or Adriatic waters. Furthermore, they had seen patrols operating in Egypt, Cyrenaica, Tripolitania and Tunisia before going to Europe where they were employed in the Aegean, Greece, Albania, Yugoslavia and Italy. They had marked their place in Special Forces' history, true to their motto 'Not by strength, by guile.'

(**Below**) Cedars of Lebanon LRDG training headquarters, a picturesque ski resort in the mountains above Beirut.

(**Opposite, above**) LRDG squadrons halt in the Sinai desert on their way to a new base at the Cedars in Lebanon. Jeeps were now their mainstay vehicle and they were mounted with .50 calibre Browning machine guns. During the Cedars training and on Leros, on different occasions, two LRDG men died in jeep accidents and several were injured.

(**Opposite, below**) LRDG troops training in the Cedars in Lebanon. They carry their heavy Bergen rucksacks and are armed with .303 Lee Enfield rifles. By late 1943, this was standard LRDG uniform and equipment on foot patrols. Lance Corporal C.A. Yaxley of T1 Patrol looks at the camera.

Lance Corporal D. Munro, T2 Patrol, poses at the Cedars with his fully-loaded British army issue Bergen rucksack. The trucks and jeeps were gone, so the men now operated as reconnaissance foot patrols, in which physical fitness had to be at the highest standard.

(**Opposite, above**) R1 Patrol resting while training at the Cedars. Front standing, Trooper J.A Franks; sitting, Sergeant M.F. Fogden, Gunner D.O. McDonald and Private C.B. McKenzie. Middle row, right: Private D.G. Dobson. Back, left: Private J.S. McIntyre, Private L. Dean and Private D.E. Wheeler. The other sitting trooper is unidentified.

(**Opposite, below**) An old Y Patrol Chevrolet 'desert warhorse' now reduced to ski field transport, identified as a B Squadron vehicle B73. Interesting that it still carries the rolled up sand mats; maybe in case it gets stuck in the snow! Note the distinctive camouflage pattern on the truck.

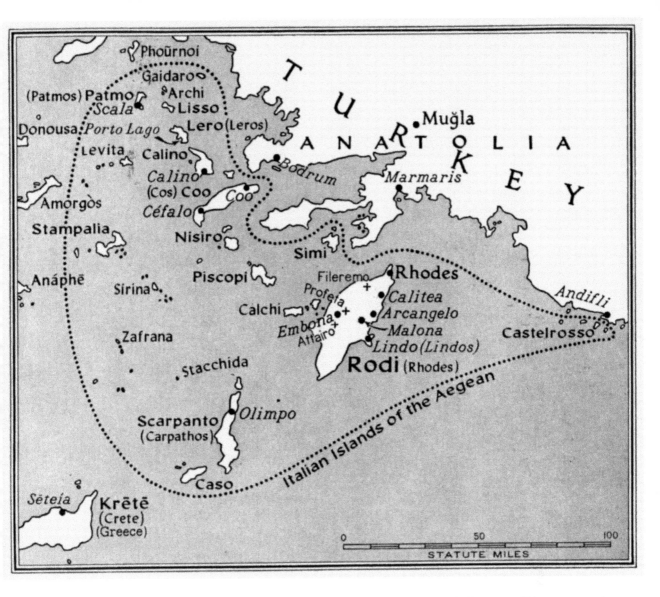

(**Opposite, above**) Sitting left, Corporal G. Weil LRDG HQ, attached to R Patrol. He was a ski instructor at the Cedars. Right, Gunner H. (Sam) Federmann, also an LRDG ski instructor. He was later killed in action while with Y Patrol in the assault on Levitha on 24 October 1943. The women are unidentified.

(**Above**) A wartime map showing the Italian islands of the Aegean in the Dodecanese. After the Italian surrender in mid-1943, for strategic reasons there was a race to occupy these islands between the German and British forces. The Italian forces had now sided with the Allies. Leros was the main base for the British and the LRDG established watchers on the outer islands. The Germans took Rhodes and Kos, among other smaller islands.

(**Opposite, below**) Kastellorizo town. On 9 September, British forces had established a base there. Consequently later in October, the town was subject to heavy raids by the Luftwaffe. Note the large caique in port and damaged German-marked seaplane.

(**Opposite, above**) Kalymnos wharf, 25 September 1943. Italian navy personnel and Greek civilians welcome the arrival of the LRDG, SBS and Commandos. The Raiding Forces were based on the island until 4 October, when due to the enemy taking Kos, they had to withdraw.

(**Opposite, below**) LRDG men on board a Greek caique. These motorized sailing vessels came in various sizes and were employed by the Levant Schooner Flotilla (LSF). They were armed and crewed by the Royal Navy and used to transport the Raiding Forces around the islands.

(**Above**) The small LSF caique LS3 transporting LRDG men. In heavy weather, the smaller vessels could be uncomfortable and cause seasickness for the landing parties on island watches.

(**Opposite, above left**) Captain C.K. ('Charlie') Saxton. He led the New Zealand T1 patrol on the successful Kythnos Island watch. Later on Leros, he was also a part of the LRDG fighting patrols. In 1938, Saxton played as a New Zealand rugby All Black. Immediately after the war, he was chosen to captain and coach the 2nd New Zealand Expeditionary Force (2 NZEF) rugby team on a successful tour of Britain and France.

(**Opposite, above right**) Lieutenant D.J. ('Jack') Aitken, commander of R1 Patrol on Naxos. Later he also oversaw the Italian battery on Mount Zuncona, Leros.

(**Opposite, below**) British Signaller Bill Smith of R1 Patrol sitting in his radio position on Mount Zuncona, Point 226. This was situated alongside the Italian PL 113 anti-aircraft battery, which was later knocked out by Ju 88 bombers. The Germans had total dominance of the air and eventually overwhelmed the British and Italian garrison troops, leading to the capitulation of Leros.

(**Above**) The bombing of Leros; a photo taken from the LRDG observation point on Zuncona. This indicates the type of difficult terrain on which the German paratroopers had to descend. Many sustained injuries landing on the rocky ground.

A GENERAL VIEW OF THE PRINCIPAL TOWN AND PORT OF LEROS. SANTA MARINA, OR LEROS, ON THE EAST COAST OF THE ISLAND, REPORTED AS HELD BY OUR FORCES ON NOVEMBER 15.

A wartime view of Santa Marina showing a typical Leros town as published in the *Illustrated London News*, 20 November 1943.

Lieutenant S.N. Eastwood of the Rhodesian S2 Patrol (left), pictured alongside his brother James. While on an intelligence-gathering mission on Kalymnos, Eastwood and his patrol were captured. However, with the help of the Greeks they later escaped the island.

Lieutenant Colonel David Lloyd Owen had a long and distinguished service as an LRDG officer. From late 1943 to the end of the war, he was the LRDG officer in command. In the post-war years he retired as a major general decorated with the CB, DSO, OBE and MC and became the chairman of the LRDG (UK) Association.

Right, Lieutenant Colonel J.R. ('Jake') Easonsmith DSO was promoted to Officer Commanding LRDG in the 1943 Aegean operations. He was a highly-respected and brave officer who was killed in action while on a night patrol during the battle for Leros. His loss was widely felt by his fellow officers and men. Left: Colonel G.L. (Guy) Prendergast DSO, who was appointed to Officer Commanding Raiding Forces, Aegean, to oversee LRDG and SBS operations. After Easonsmith was killed, Prendergast resumed direct command over the Group, narrowly escaping Leros after the defeat.

T and R Patrol members while on leave in Beirut in 1943. Left: Private R.E.J. Hare, Private T. Collins, Gunner J.R. ('Ian') Gold and Private T.R. McLelland. Collins went on to serve on Mount Scumbarda overseeing the coastal guns on Leros. Gold and McLelland were later captured in the assault on Levitha in October 1943.

(**Opposite, above**) Stuka bombing of Leros as recorded in *The Sphere* magazine of 11 December 1943. It also shows the type of landscape over which the battle was fought.

(**Opposite, below**) A dramatic artist's impression of the German attack of Leros, as illustrated in *The Sphere* magazine in December 1943. It shows the chaos of the action, with the defenders shooting at the Stukas and Ju 52s discharging paratroopers. One observer described what he saw as follows: 'The sight of these coloured chutes billowing out as they slowly came down made quite a beautiful picture. In firing on them we used largely tracer ammunition, which gave the whole scene the aspect of some wizard fair!' The drawing reflects his comment.

(**Right**) Captain J.R. Olivey MC, a very capable and fearless patrol leader. He commanded his fellow Rhodesians of S Patrol in the difficult action on Clidi. A month earlier, he also led the assault on Levitha, but was only one of a handful who escaped the island following the defeat. However, he was captured after the fall of Leros, although he later escaped in Greece and eventually returned home. For his gallant work in the Clidi action, he was awarded a Bar to the Military Cross he received in North Africa in 1941.

(**Below**) The San Giorgio coastal gun battery in action, situated on the heights of Point 334/Scumbarda. Second Lieutenant R.F. White and men of R2 Patrol oversaw the Italian gun position. Despite regular air attacks, most of the guns at this battery remained in action until the final day of the battle, when the patrol had to escape the island.

(**Above**) Italian Marines serving a 152mm naval coastal defence gun. They initially undertook good work against the enemy landings, but most of the positions on the Leros heights were eventually knocked out by Stuka Ju 87 and Ju 88 air attacks. Five LRDG patrols were assigned to the gun battery positions, employing the heights as coastal observation points but also to stiffen the morale of their new allies, ensuring the guns and their crews performed effectively.

(**Opposite, above**) San Giorgio Battery, Point 334/Scumbarda. The aftermath of a Stuka attack where a small bomb exploded close to the entrance of one of the patrol's shelter caves damaging radio equipment. Second Lieutenant R.F. White and his men watch the sky for any further aircraft overhead. Note the coastal gun in the background.

(**Opposite, below**) Second Lieutenant White's escape party from Leros to Turkey. On their way, they stopped at the small island of Farmakonisi. There they made a mast from a small tree and created a sail from an army tent. The photo shows them departing the island on the evening of 17 November 1943.

Frank White's escape party rest for a meal after landing on the Turkish coast on the morning of 18 November. From left: Second Lieutenant R.F. White, Lieutenant G.V. Pavlides, Gunner W. Morrison, Gunner G.F. McDowell(?) and Trooper S. Kerr.

A simple map of Leros taken from a wartime illustration in the *Daily Telegraph* newspaper.

LRDG Leros escapees gather on the wharf in Turkey before departing by ship to Haifa. Though a poor-quality photo, it is a good study of the state of the men after their escape. Standing left: Second Lieutenant F.R. White with his Bergen rucksack.

(**Opposite, above**) Escapees from Leros on a minesweeper sailing from Turkey to Palestine. From left: Sergeant J.L.D. Davis, Lance Corporal C.A. Yaxley, Sergeant M.D. Richardson, Lance Corporal J.H.E. Taylor and Captain C.K. Saxton (smiling, right rear).

(**Opposite, below**) Captioned on the back of the original photo: 'Dannie Evans and Paddy, T1 radio operators.' They were on their way to Haifa after escaping Leros. A .303 Lewis gun is mounted behind them. Note on the right, an exhausted Italian soldier sleeps.

(**Left**) LRDG Captain A.M. Greenwood returned to Leros after the defeat to search for British escapees. He disguised himself as a Greek peasant to enable him to walk freely around occupied Leros while looking for men in hiding. Greenwood was awarded the Military Cross and Mentioned in Dispatches for his service in the Mediterranean theatre.

(**Above**) Group photo of LRDG officers at Azzib, Christmas 1943. Back row, left to right: Alan Denniff, Archie Gibson, George Pavlides, Merv Cross, Moir Stormonth-Darling, Charles Hall, unknown, Gordon Rowbottom, Michael Parsons, Ron Tinker, Ashley Greenwood, Joe Braithwaite and F.T. McMahon. Front, left to right: Cecil 'Jacko' Jackson, Bill Armstrong, Charles Saxton, Jack Aitken, Arthur Stokes and Trevor Barker (LRDG pilot).

(**Opposite, above**) Christmas 1943. Left: New Zealand (A) Squadron members Trooper S. Kerr and Private T. Collins hold up a blanket decorated with cotton wool art. It was presented as a farewell gift from the Rhodesians to the New Zealanders, wishing them '*Kia Ora*', (a Maori greeting meaning 'Good health') and 'Happy Days' as they disband from the LRDG.

(**Opposite, below**) Leonard Marsland Gander of the *Daily Telegraph* was the only British war correspondent on Leros. His independent reporting provided a dramatic insight into the island battle. A vivid headline describing the action from the *Egyptian Mail*, 20 November 1943.

Leros Battle 'Like A Highly Improbable Film'

MARSLAND GANDER of the "Daily Telegraph," who was the only War Correspondent on the island, tells the human story behind the battle.

Marsland Gander

WE stepped from the motor launch on to the wooden jetty in Alinda Bay, thankful to be off dangerous waters, only to come creeping into Alinda Bay. What did "A" do then?

We clumped on bare wooden floors, stumbling over recumbent figures. Somebody woke and said that there were spare camp beds on the first floor if we cared to use them. Sleep was impossible. All night the hum of aircraft filled the air. Crichton thought they were our own transports dropping supplies and we had certainly seen soldiers carrying parachutes

LANDINGS PAID US DIVIDENDS

hauled up the 600-foot mountain side in cans from the valley. When the parachutists seized the island's central waist half our wells were no longer available and we had to rely on those in the Portolago area. So after the first day there was no washing or shaving and the drinking water had to be conserved. Before leaving for Leros we had been given white and green sterilising tablets for the water but in the heat of

the weapon pit beside me. "Let me have a crack," he urged the gunner. He fired over the bay at the Ju's and I saw one with a parachute dragging behind burst into flames and dive into the bay. Another Ju dropped all the parachutists in the sea where transitory circles marked their several graves.

"It's like duck shooting. You aim just ahead," said the captain and he shouted gleefully as sparks flew from another Ju which went off in a shallow dive.

Hanging Like Marionettes

With the naked eye we could see the parachutists swing helpless on their cords like marionettes. Through glasses some could be seen hanging on telegraph wires and trees and others lay prone on the ground as if shot in the air or injured

manded the password.

As like as not we didn't know it but a few well known English expletives were just as good. At one point this road was overlooked by snipers, at another it came under mortar fire. So it was a case of running creeping and hiding over some stretches. At intervals when the bombs came near we threw ourselves flat.

But by far my biggest shock was one morning when scrambling down the mountain side I saw a party of Germans marching round the corner of the road below. Then with relief I noticed a British sergeant with fixed bayonet following them jauntily. They were prisoners. As an example of the troops' spirit I recall one evening when our little group at the tunnel entrance, weary after the day's bombing but relieved that it had ceased for the moment, burst spontaneously into a chorus: "She'll come rolling

Notes

Notes

Notes

Notes

Notes

Notes

Notes

Notes

Notes